Mike's World
The Life of Mike Myers

D1007355

Martin Knelman

FIREFLY BOOKS

A FIREFLY BOOK

Published by Firefly Books Ltd. 2003

First printing

Publisher Cataloguing-in-Publication Data (U.S.)
(Library of Congress Standards)

Knelman, Martin.
   Mike's world : the life of Mike Myers / by Martin
Knelman.
[268] p. : col. photos. ; cm.
Includes bibliographical references and index.
Summary: A biography of the comic actor who became
popular on "Saturday Night Live" and went on to star
in such movies as "Wayne's World" and "Austin
Powers: International Man of Mystery."
ISBN 1-55297-661-0 (pbk.)
1. Myers, Mike, 1963–. 2. Comedians—Canada—
Biography.   3. Motion picture actors and actresses—
Canada—Biography. I. Title.
792.7/ 028/ 092 B 21   PN2308.M94.K64 2003

Photo credits:
Front cover: Shooting Star (main image)
Everett Collection/Magma

Published in the United States in 2003 by
Firefly Books (U.S.) Inc.
P.O. Box 1338, Ellicott Station
Buffalo, New York 14205

Printed in Canada

In memory of Urjo Kareda (1944–2001),
whose laughter still reverberates

CONTENTS

INTRODUCTION

Scar-ber-i-a they called it, stretching out the syllables in mock agony to describe the horrors of life in Scarborough, on the fringes of Toronto. But Mike Myers had a remarkably happy childhood there, and for years he was fondly known to some people as the funniest guy ever to come out of a basement recreation room in Scarborough. His route to fairy tale success carried him from Second City stages in Toronto and Chicago to *Saturday Night Live* in New York to Hollywood triumphs playing Wayne Campbell and Austin Powers—characters from an imagination

7

nurtured during his Scarborough childhood.

But during the summer of 2000, Myers became famous in an entirely different way. He became the star and victim of an offscreen Hollywood melodrama known as "Dietergate." Myers had decided that a new movie he had been writing as a vehicle for himself, *Sprockets*, was not ready to go before the cameras. As a result, he found himself the latest big name on a list of dubious distinction: movie celebrities vilified and demonized for being at the center of a scandal.

This was by no means the first time in Hollywood history that something like this had happened, although few of Mike Myers's fans would likely have memories stretching back to those earlier incidents, some going back as long as 75 years.

Over the years, the pattern has been familiar. A big star becomes embroiled in controversy and is considered a threat to the Hollywood establishment. Among the power brokers, a consensus emerges that this star has to be punished, humiliated and taught a lesson. The instrument for this justice is usually to leak damaging information, or disinformation, to the media—especially the most powerful within the Hollywood gossip machine.

In the mid-1920s, another famous comedian, Fatty Arbuckle, became the most tragic victim of this nasty process. His career was destroyed as a result of what became known as "the case of the wild party." A girl attending that party became ill and died a few days later. Arbuckle was arrested for her murder on extremely flimsy evidence. Although Arbuckle was almost certainly innocent (he was eventually acquitted), he was offered up as a sacrifice by Hollywood's rich and powerful, afraid of a moral-majority backlash that might cripple the whole entertainment industry.

In 1941 it was the young Orson Welles who was virtually driven out of Hollywood. He'd had the audacity to make a movie called *Citizen Kane*—which only years later became known as the greatest American movie of all time. But in 1941, what mattered was the scandalous matter of William Randolph Hearst, who was clearly the model for the movie's deeply unflattering portrayal of a media baron called Charles Foster Kane. Since Hearst was in a position to do serious damage to Hollywood, he had to be placated. Hearst gossip columnist Louella Parsons led the charge. The consequences: *Citizen Kane* got lousy distribution, lost money and was given only one measly Academy Award.

Next it was Ingrid Bergman's turn. Her crime? She left her husband and ran off with the famous Italian director Roberto Rosellini. Her punishment: She was *persona non grata* in Hollywood for a decade.

Of course, the greatest shame in Hollywood history

came in the 1940s and 1950s with the "Red Scare" and the blacklist. Many careers were destroyed because somebody sometime whispered that somebody might once have been a Communist.

MIKE MYERS WAS BY NATURE a painfully shy and introverted person, not the extroverted clown he turns into when performing. And he was a perfectionist obsessed with details. So it was hardly surprising some people considered him moody and difficult to work with. But then being moody and difficult is character-istic of many movie stars, and they aren't all portrayed in the media as demonic monsters.

So what did Mike Myers do to earn the mudsling-ing that came his way in the summer of 2000? Well, he walked away from a movie that his partners— Universal Studios and Imagine Entertainment—felt sure was going to make a lot of money. The movie he backed out of, *Sprockets*, was about Dieter, one of his celebrated *Saturday Night Live* characters. Universal launched a lawsuit that turned so nasty it involved private detectives and character assassination.

You might think moviegoers would regard it as heroic that somebody would actually give up a $20 million paycheck just because he thought the script wasn't ready and he didn't want to be part of a bad movie—didn't want his fans to be suckered into paying $12 for a stinker. The quality of Hollywood comedies might be much higher if a few other movie stars would do the same.

Yet somehow Myers wound up being portrayed as the villain—the overpaid, temperamental brat—and came away with enough negative press to fill a large scrapbook—most notably a long and notoriously unflattering profile in *Vanity Fair* in which many people who had worked with Myers over the years were allowed to speak venomously and in some cases anonymously.

Here's what Hollywood found really scary about Myers: he couldn't be trusted because in the end, he didn't care that much about money. True, he had fought tenaciously to get his fee up to more than $20 million. Yet he was prepared to give up even that staggering an amount of money for one reason. Mike's greatest fear—going back to his Scarborough child-hood and the "rules of the game" he learned from his father—was not being funny enough. Since he felt *Sprockets* wasn't going to be funny enough, no amount of money could persuade him to do it.

He had reason to be wary. Earlier in his career, he had learned about the perils of not being funny enough. As a result, he had watched in dismay as his career went into turnaround.

In 1993, after his second *Wayne's World* movie and

the misconceived *So I Married an Axe Murderer* both flopped, Myers vanished from Hollywood's radar screen for several years.

That same year, Mike's beloved father, Eric Myers, died after a long ordeal with Alzheimer's. It was Eric, the *Encyclopaedia Britannica* salesman from Liverpool, who had elevated the importance of being silly and made it an integral part of his personal values.

Eric told Mike and his two older brothers silliness was a state of grace.

When Eric died, Mike's heart was broken, and he just didn't feel like working. Nothing seemed funny.

So he dropped out for a while.

Out of that downtime came the inspiration for his comeback vehicle, *Austin Powers: International Man of Mystery*. The way he saw it, *Austin Powers* was a tribute to his father and a spoofy homage to the decade when Mike was born—the 1960s.

The rest is showbiz history. *Austin Powers: International Man of Mystery* was the big summer hit in 1997. And *Austin Powers: The Spy Who Shagged Me* was an even bigger hit in the summer of 1999.

It turned out that not even the "Dietergate" scandal could derail Mike's career. Eventually the legal battle was settled through an out-of-court deal negotiated by DreamWorks SKG boss Jeffrey Katzenberg, whose studio was about to release the animated movie

Shrek—in which Myers supplied the voice of the cartoon ogre.

Just two years after his vilification and demonization, Mike Myers earned forgiveness. *Goldmember*, the third installment of the *Austin Powers* movies, was the big comedy hit of the 2002 summer season pulling in $287.9 million at the box office. And Myers himself seemed blessed with a Midas touch. He was now considered not only funny and bankable; he had also proved to be a survivor of one of the highest-profile character assassinations in movie history.

In July Myers had his hand and footprints immortalized in the cement on the Walk of Fame in front of Mann's Chinese Theatre in Hollywood. Three months later came an honor that was closer to home. A Toronto street in his old Scarborough neighborhood (near Lawrence Avenue and Kennedy Road) was named Mike Myers Drive.

When he first heard about it, Mike was thrilled because "Scarborough has helped to shape who I am." But then, he adds, "I was told it doesn't mean I actually own the street. Well, even if I can't levy taxes or start my own army, it's still pretty cool."

1

APRIL FOOLS

On APRIL FOOL'S DAY, 2001, a group of fans waited on the sidewalk outside the stage door of the Winter Garden Theatre in downtown Toronto. One of them was clutching an Austin Powers action figure.

It was a cold Sunday night, with spring still only a rumor.

Inside the theater, the performance about to begin was billed as *An Evening with Funny Canadians*. This was to be a one-time panel discussion featuring noted comedians, and the purpose of the exercise was to raise scholarship money so funny people could enroll in the comedy program at Humber College and be turned into professional comedians.

The lineup of panelists included Dave Foley and Kevin McDonald of the *Kids in the Hall* comedy troupe, as well as Colin Mochrie, star of the popular TV comedy series *Whose Line Is It Anyway?*

But the real cause of the buzz inside the theater and on the street was that one of the panelists was Mike Myers, the funniest and most beloved dude ever to emerge from a basement in Scarborough.

It was quite a coup for Humber to get him, but there were a few good reasons Myers said yes.

Reason one: The guy who was asking was his former Second City mentor, Allan Guttman, who was now director of the comedy program at Humber.

Reason two: The event happened to coincide with the birthday of Mike's mother, so he was happy to be in Toronto for the weekend.

Reason three: With both a writers' and an actors' strike looming in Hollywood, there was less pressure to meet script deadlines for future movies.

Reason four: Six months after the publication of a sensationally unfavorable article in *Vanity Fair* magazine, Mike was still doing damage control, trying to convince people he wasn't really the ruthless, ungrateful monster portrayed in the article—the kind of guy who achieved stardom at the expense of ex-colleagues by failing to give them credit for the crucial contributions they had made to his act.

What better place to start improving his image than in his hometown? For Mike, giving a boost to Humber was a way to demonstrate that he was a caring person who hadn't forgotten where he came from or the people who helped him become a star.

And only the previous week, Mike had generated another wave of nasty publicity at the Academy Awards presentation in Los Angeles. Presenting an award for sound, he mangled the names of nominees and made light of the fact that, in his view, no one would remember who had won the Oscar in this category. His routine was meant to be funny, but so many people were outraged that the Academy issued an official apology.

Now Mike was back in Toronto, at least for a few days, which he might have considered a safe haven—cozily familiar territory, where he liked to play hockey with friends at Ramsden Park, cheer for his beloved Maple Leafs as they battled National Hockey League rivals, drink caffe latte at Starbucks and quaff beer with friends at his favorite English pub, the Duke of York on Prince Arthur Avenue. In Toronto, surely, Mike would be loved and understood, and regarded as a regular guy.

Since the *Vanity Fair* article had blackened his name, Mike had been spending a lot of time on the phone, calling old friends from his formative days in the 1980s at Toronto's Second City club to see if they were harboring any resentments and to make peace if they were.

For the Humber comedy benefit, most of the other panelists had arrived on time at 7:15 P.M., three-quarters of an hour before they were due to go on stage to talk about why Canadians are so funny.

Among those milling about exchanging greetings, drinking bottled water and pretending not to be nervous: moderator Ralph Benmergui, Yuk Yuk's comedy club owner Mark Breslin and veteran Second City comedienne Robin Duke.

Everyone was trying to seem cool, but beyond that you could sense a distinct tension about one participant who was conspicuously late.

Fifteen minutes before showtime, a stretch limo pulled up. Mike Myers emerged from the car with his wife, Robin Ruzan, and his personal assistant—taking time to sign autographs.

Stepping off the elevator 10 minutes later, he was warmly greeted by Humber staff.

But could this really be the lovably extroverted clown who had parlayed his gift for creating zany characters into celebrity on *Saturday Night Live* and then went on to Hollywood megastardom with two *Wayne's World* movies and two *Austin Powers* movies?

Could this be the outgoing, unpretentious regular guy who liked to hang out at Starbucks and go to Leafs games?

Wary and unsmiling, Humber's special guest seemed, in the words of Linda Richman, a little *verklempt* (a Yiddish word meaning "overcome by emotion"). Indeed, he was behaving less like the most popular funnyman on the big screen than like his edgy doppelganger. You might call him Dr. Nervous.

He had a carefully put together casual look, highlighted by a pullover sweater and a hairdo that one derisive onlooker said made him look like a squeegee kid.

"Is there a room for us to go to?" Myers inquired curtly, before disappearing into his dressing room.

He had little to say to his fellow panelists, but as Breslin put it: "We were all in a world of our own and preoccupied the way people are before a show starts."

And as everyone who has spent time hanging around comedians knows, nervousness, insecurity, paranoia and depressive personalities go with the territory.

Still, when he emerged from his dressing room, Mike tried to lighten the mood by offering everyone goodies—gourmet chocolate truffles. Most of his colleagues were too nervous to eat chocolates.

When asked by Mark Lappano, Humber's logistics manager, whether he was feeling OK, Myers replied:

"To tell you the truth, Mark, I'm feeling a little bagged." It was, he explained, a combination of the jet lag (after flying in from Los Angeles) and the changeover from standard to daylight saving time. "I'm just trying to save some energy for the show," he told Lappano.

This is how it goes when you're not just another overripe teenager hanging out in a suburban Toronto rec room, but a movie star who's just moved beyond the fabled $20-million club by signing to make *Austin Powers 3* (aka *Goldmember*) for $25 million (U.S.).

The latest Myers visit to his hometown was veiled in secrecy, marked by excruciating negotations between Humber officials and members of Mike's staff, some of whom seemed to be tripping over others.

Humber had been approached by TV producers who wanted to tape the benefit evening for telecast. At first, Myers and his people said that would be fine. Humber officials were looking forward to making a large sum of money from the taping. Then came word from Myers, Inc. that they couldn't grant permission after all. The reason: Mike's settlement with Universal included complicated legal restrictions that meant he would have to get special permission for the taping, and the procedure involved jumping through so many hoops, it just wasn't worth it.

But Mike felt so guilty about this twist, and was so eager to be the perfect benefactor, that he wrote a personal check to make up for the income Humber would lose through not being able to tape the show.

For days and weeks there was much confusion about how long Myers was going to be in town, where he would be staying and whether he would be able to do any interviews to promote the event.

In the end Mike and Robin flew in on Friday, March 30, and stayed for three nights at the Four Seasons Hotel in Yorkville, where they were registered under a phony name. (Humber had been offered a free suite at another luxury hotel, but Myers insisted on the Four Seasons.)

On Saturday night, they attended a family party to celebrate the birthday of Mike's mother, Alice (aka Bunny).

On Sunday evening, the minute the panelists came on stage to be introduced, almost 15 minutes late, Dr. Nervous, who had been deflating the mood backstage, was suddenly replaced by a zany extrovert—Toronto's most beloved clown.

Spotting an Austin Powers look-alike wearing a red suit in the front row, Myers impulsively jumped off the stage and changed seats with the fan.

A few minutes later, when the film clips began, out of view of the panelists, he jumped up and lay on his back on the stage floor to watch the clip.

But Myers had things on his mind besides clowning

around. He had a few solemn remarks to make about
comedy and the Canadian identity—earnest enough
to earn him a sarcastic review from one Toronto journalist, who said Mike came across like a homeroom
teacher trying to get the class ready for midterm
exams.

"I think it's interesting that all of us talk about being
Canadian in reference to the United States," Mike
remarked. "There's no kind of reason for us to exist,"
he observed. "We're in a country that started with a
mission statement . . . I love being from Canada, and
I love Canadian things. If you go to Europe, you can
spot a Canadian at a hundred paces. But we don't seem
to have a national cuisine. And I don't know why we
don't have one popular movie (about being Canadian)
like the Québécois have *Les Boys*."

Myers became most animated when he got on to
the subject of Pierre Trudeau, whom he called a great
man.

Before the show was over, he also joined an improvisational sketch, taking the role of the Devil's
Advocate.

And he fielded some questions from the audience—
sounding at one point a bit curmudgeonly. Asked
whether he would prefer to be Superman or James
Bond, Mike complained: "Why the same questions all
the time? Change the questions, people!"

After the show, Mike lingered for a surprisingly long time signing autographs for his fans—by which time his wife, Robin, was asking Humber dean Joe Kertes to help extricate her husband because they had to leave.

Around midnight they joined Mochrie and his wife, Debra McGrath (who had performed with Myers in Second City stage shows in the late 1980s), at Jeremiah Bullfrog, a pub on Queen Street West. They were joined by a few mutual friends and several students from Humber's comedy department.

After that, it was back to the Four Seasons suite for the $25-million man and his wife.

Here in Toronto's upscale Yorkville area, Mike was closing his eyes less than a 30 minute drive from the Sheppard-and-Pharmacy section of Scarborough where he'd grown up three decades earlier; and only a short walk from the flat over a Korean fruit store near Bathurst and Bloor where he'd lived in the late 1980s while cavorting at Second City. But now thanks to two *Wayne's World* movies and two *Austin Powers* movies, he seemed to be living on another planet.

Just call him Mike Myers, International Man of Mystery.

2

SCARBERIA

THOUGH MIKE MYERS WAS BORN IN CANADA and
grew up in Scarborough, a suburban offshoot of
Toronto, his parents made the Myers home a shrine to
all things Liverpudlian. It was almost as if Eric and
Alice wanted to deny they had ever left the Old Swan
district of Liverpool and moved across the Atlantic in
search of a more prosperous life.

Born in 1922, Eric Myers had served with the Royal
Engineers in World War II, mostly as an army cook.
Then at Dunlop, the tire company, he had worked his
way up from the shop floor, taking night classes and

24

earning a promotion to management. As Mike would boast in interviews years later, that was a gargantuan, heroic feat in the Liverpool of the 1950s—the equivalent of a private becoming a general.

Eric met Alice, a trained actress, when they were both doing amateur dramatics in Liverpool. She had also served in World War II—working in an underground bunker for the Royal Air Force in Maidstone, Kent. After the war, she had studied acting at the London Academy of Dramatic Art.

Alice's father was a strong believer in the doctrine of self-improvement, and he'd taught Alice that just because you were born into the working class didn't mean you couldn't rise above it. Alice was always pushing herself and others to do better and rise to a higher station in life. That's why the chance to move to Canada struck her as a tremendous opportunity.

By the time Eric and Alice crossed the Atlantic Ocean in 1956—a year after their marriage—they were both over 30, and eager to start a new life. (Decades later, Mike would post in his home office a blown-up photo of his parents boarding the boat.) Canada was seeking immigrants at the time; Eric and Alice responded to a newspaper advertisement. It was a yen for adventure, as well as the promise of economic improvement, that led them to move. But once in Toronto, they kept the spirit of Liverpool alive in their household as they moved from one place to another—starting with an apartment on Eccleston Drive near the intersection of Toronto's Don Valley Parkway and Eglinton Avenue, then going to Don Mills Road near the Fairview Mall.

And the language they spoke was not quite Canadian vernacular; it was what their youngest son would later describe as "Liverpoolese." Indeed, to the ears of the young Michael Myers (as he was known throughout his childhood), the thick accent of his parents set them apart from everyone else in Scarborough and left him with the definite impression he must be related to the Beatles, who were conquering the world for the glory of Liverpool around the time he was born. John, Paul, George and Ringo were the only people Michael and his brothers knew of who talked the same way Eric and Alice did.

Relatives of Eric and Alice seemed to think they had moved to a wilderness frontier, and got into the habit of sending the pioneer branch of the family care packages of clothing with such items as Beatles boots and Beatles suits. And though Toronto was soon to become one of the most prosperous, ambitious and lively cities in North America, in a sense Eric and Alice had indeed moved to the frontier.

They settled in Scarborough in a patch of suburbia that had been developed only since the end of the

World War II. They were perched at the place where the largest and most sophisticated city in English Canada bumped up against the vast spaces of what had until recently been farmland.

As the journalist and critic Robert Fulford has remarked, Toronto is best understood as a series of underground secrets: from the four-mile-long downtown tunnel system that links hotels, banks and office towers, to the magnificent system of ravines that snakes its way through the northeast part of the city, taking you by surprise as you explore the hidden trails lurking just beyond some of its prettier middle-class neighborhoods.

This hidden topography is a defining quality of Toronto and gives it a private identity. Ravines are to Toronto, according to Fulford, what canals are to Venice.

And they provide a flip side to the suburban blight that makes up much of the landscape in the kind of instant new environment where Eric and Alice settled along with thousands of other hopeful newcomers. Driving around the main streets of Scarborough and North York, it might seem as if Factory Carpet outlets, doughnut shops and expressways set the aesthetic standards. Yet the children who grew up in the cheap cookie-cutter postwar townhouses quickly came to understand that there were patches of enchantment all around them—magical forests that suddenly revealed themselves at the back of unsightly apartment buildings.

Eric Myers made a living by selling the *Encyclopaedia Britannica* door to door, and in 1957 he was given a ring for being the company's top salesman of the year. Alice worked at a bank. Later on, Eric sold insurance for the Independent Order of Foresters, and Alice became a data processor for a chemical company that made aerosol products.

Their first child, Peter, was born in 1959. A second son, Paul, was born three years later. Michael, the youngest of Eric and Alice's three sons, was born on May 25, 1963.

The way he would remember it in interviews years later, the family environment was jolly. Eric and Alice had a happy marriage. And Eric's only tyrannical tendency was his insistence that nothing in life was more important than comedy (especially British comedy) and a sense of humor. He would wake his boys up late at night if there was a chance to introduce them to a film starring one of the great British comic actors, Peter Sellers or Alec Guinness. And to Eric it would be unthinkable to miss the *Goon Show, Benny Hill* or *Monty Python's Flying Circus*. Peter Cook and Dudley Moore from *Beyond the Fringe* were also among his heroes.

Although Alice became a Canadian citizen, Eric never did; he always remained a staunch Englishman who had somehow, unaccountably, strayed off the island. Eric Myers was living proof that, as his son would put it years later, "There is no one more English than an Englishman who no longer lives in England."

Eric even refused to eat pineapple on the grounds that it was Hawaiians who'd killed one of his favorite British heroes, Captain Cook. It didn't matter that this had happened 300 years ago, and that the Hawaiians had established a good track record more recently.

As the youngest of three boys, Mike Myers recalls being the family punching bag. "I got peed on a lot," he explained in an interview on the TV program *Inside the Actors Studio*. His older brothers thought they were hilarious—and so did Michael. The way he remembers it, Paul and Peter taunted him mercilessly, and made him the ongoing victim of their shenanigans.

Once, he told *Rolling Stone* magazine, they stripped him naked and threw him into the hallway of their apartment building. He was rescued by a kindly neighbor—a tiny East Indian woman whose sari was just the right size for Michael.

It was Peter who introduced Michael to the imagined countries of Snotavia Roughnicia, which became part of his fantasy world. His preoccupation with toy soldiers would continue into adulthood.

Although the Myers house was happy, it was also a place of extreme emotional restraint. Years later, Mike explained: "I have a very well-maintained proximic bubble. Much to the the amusement and frustration of my New York Jewish wife and her family, I'm not a big hugger. I'm a very shy person. Ultimately it's not only being Canadian, but from growing up in a British-Canadian house. You don't cry a lot—you tend to shake hands and not hug."

Eric Myers looked a little like Peter Sellers, and as far as Eric was concerned, the art of silliness in English humor was for him almost a religious calling. He would say silliness was an underrated art form and a state of grace. He taught his sons to have no inhibitions, encouraging them to be the architects of their own embarrassment.

Eric's belief in comedy as a way of life was much more important to him than the work he did to support the family. He was constantly perplexed by the North American habit of asking people what they did for a living, as if that defined them. The fact that Eric made his living as a salesman was, to his mind, incidental to his true identity. And so when he was asked what he did, Eric liked to give a silly answer. He would say he made the metal tips on shoelaces. Or that he played the bongo drums on the theme song of *Mission Impossible*. Or that he was the ambassador to

Guatemala.

"I liked how the house felt when a good comedy was on," Eric's youngest son explained years later. My dad was a big laugher, and I liked the feeling of a room laughing."

Eric drank 10 cups of tea a day, always standing up, never sitting down. "D'ya wanna cupatea, lad?" he would ask whichever of his sons happened to be around. He even loved to make tea part of his favorite game of toy soldiers, banging a spoon against his teacup. The house was full of Eric's gleeful laugh as he turned even a burp into a comedy routine with remarks like: "Sweet mystery of life, I'm so glad I found you."

Eric's utopian vision of England was put to the test in 1974, when the whole Myers family took a trip to the mother country. They had gone back previously to christen Peter and Paul, but they didn't get around to it in Michael's case—and he never was christened. Making his first trip across the Atlantic at age 11, Michael was startled to discover that England was not quite the vastly superior paradise he had heard about from Eric. "The phones sounded weird, and the cars drove on the wrong side of the road," he told Chris Heath of *Rolling Stone* in 1999. "I was thinking, 'Oh, come on, now—you're just going out of your way to be different.'"

Probably the main impact of the trip to England was that it made the entire family realize how much they actually enjoyed living in Canada. Michael was delighted to return to Scarborough.

Eric and Alice liked to go out dancing on Saturday nights, leaving their three sons at home. The boys loved having the house to themselves. They would check the TV listings, hoping to catch a James Bond movie or a Matt Helm film. Or they would watch the National Hockey League game on CBC, usually telecast live from Maple Leaf Gardens and featuring Michael's beloved Toronto Maple Leafs.

Part of the preparation ritual for an evening's entertainment in the basement was to lay out vast quantities of junk food: Grand Prix Cola, Dominion potato chips, Cherry Blossom chocolates. Indeed, throughout his boyhood, Michael spent countless hours fooling around in the basement rec room with his brothers. And years later, his memories of those nights would inspire him to create *Wayne's World*.

One of the friends who hung around in the basement with Michael sharing banter was David Mackenzie, on whom Wayne's sidekick, Garth, was said to be modeled.

Like many other basement rec rooms in Scarborough, the Myers' had wood paneling and old furniture that in a previous incarnation had been the good stuff in the living room.

In the eyes of his parents and brothers, Michael was the least funny member of the family. Alice sometimes told him: "Your brothers are the funny ones, Michael, but you're not. Don't even try, because you'll just get frustrated. Just sit and laugh with the rest of us."

Nevertheless, Michael began performing at what he would later describe as "a hideously young age." As far back as he could remember, it was what he wanted to do. He would put on shows for the local kids, making them laugh with his mime routines and dancing along to a TV variety show called *Pig and Whistle*.

Alice had taken her youngest son for dancing lessons, and at the age of eight, he was invited to perform a jazz dance for a Datsun commercial. As a schoolboy he wound up doing about 17 commercials, including one for Kit Kat candy bars, one for Kmart discount department stores, one for Kraft cheese and another for Pepsi. Typically, Eric would accompany Michael to auditions—and write notes asking to have him let out of school. And Alice would offer advice from her years of drama school: "Eyes and teeth, Michael! Play to the exit lights!"

According to Alice, there was more to performing than being funny. "Play your cards right and you could be the next Ken Barry," she urged. "Now that's a triple threat."

She was referring to the singing, dancing and acting prowess of the man known as Larry Storch's commanding officer on the show *F Troop*. Young Michael was a bit daunted by the expectation that he had to sing and dance, as well as create comedy characters.

No one in the family seemed to find it amazing that Michael got almost every gig he auditioned for. They just assumed that was normal.

When he was about 11 years old, Michael did a commercial for British Columbia Hydro Electric with a rising comedy actress named Gilda Radner. The premise was that hydroelectricity was cheaper than ever. They had to dance in the style of the 1950s. She played his mother, and during the course of the four-day shoot, Michael fell in love with Gilda (as almost everyone who ever worked with her did). As a result, his older brothers taunted him, calling him "sucky baby."

About a year after doing the commercial, Michael was astonished to see Gilda on a new late-night TV comedy show called *Saturday Night Live*. One of his brothers told him, "Hey, your girlfriend is on this new show." Michael, then 12, immediately announced that one day he was going to be appearing on *Saturday Night Live*. Peter and Paul got a big laugh out of the notion that their little brother would one day be performing on *SNL*.

But the work kept coming. On one occasion, Michael was flown to Hollywood to do a commercial for Wrigley's Spearmint Gum. He played a kid at camp who just loved chewing gum. One of the key bits of dialogue was the line: "It looks like you've graduated to the Big Stick."

That resulted in a lot of teasing from the other kids at school, but Michael would shrug and say he was laughing all the way to the bank.

Michael was also making the important leap from doing commercials to appearing in less lucrative but more prestigious TV-drama productions—although he had no formal training.

His first dramatic role was with Donald Sutherland in a TV production about the inventor of mobile blood transfusions. Michael was cast as the boy who lived next door to the hero. The most memorable part of the experience was that the producer and director allowed him to improvise with Sutherland.

Next, Michael landed a guest role in an episode of the CBC's most popular situation comedy series of all time, *King of Kensington*, starring Al Waxman as Larry King, a good-hearted slob who owns a variety store.

Myers played a budding con artist named Ariel who is running a phony raffle-tickets operation with the profits allegedly going to underprivileged boys. But Larry's mother (played by Helene Winston) gets a whiff of something not quite kosher.

Larry, being a sweetheart, gets in touch with Ariel's mother and winds up hiring her. But trying to give both mother and son a break, he sets himself up to get swindled.

As the unrepentant Ariel, a pint-sized, sullen delinquent, Michael Myers made an extremely respectable debut.

He was less fortunate in the case of a half-hour 1978 CBC children's special called *Range Rider and the Calgary Kid*. It was a bizarre, spoofy western that attempted to strike a comic-book flavor, including low-tech special effects, all on a shoestring budget.

"Even while we were in the middle of it, I kept thinking, 'I can't believe they really want to do this,'" recalls David Ferry, who co-starred along with such other well-known Toronto stage performers as Nancy Dolman and Ken James.

"It was a very quick shoot and Mike was a sweet kid. Things were a bit chaotic, so Nancy and I tried to protect Mike and take care of him, as if we were his big sister and brother. We chuckled a lot about how cheesy the production was."

Once he reached adolescence, Michael's work opportunities dwindled a bit, partly because he developed dreadful acne and felt painfully self-conscious about it. As a young teenager, Michael had to come to terms with the fact that he was never going to be tall or strikingly handsome. He'd have to get by on charm and talent.

Meanwhile he was developing a taste for cultural experiences besides the ones that Eric was promoting. These included listening to the rock group Queen and reading Kurt Vonnegut novels. And when he had his sexual initation, the first person he told about it was his brother Paul.

"It was a Leafs-win-the-Stanley-Cup situation," Mike would recall in an interview with *Rolling Stone* years later. "I felt matriculated."

Wheels provided exciting new access to experiences beyond his basement and his neighborhood. When Peter got his first car, the Myers brothers would go out to McDonald's at Warden and Sheppard, or the Tim Hortons doughnut shop to the west on Sheppard. They would play loud rock music while driving around.

When Mike was in high school, one of his friends had a brown Dodge with a vomit stain on the side. They discovered that a short expressway trip down the Don Valley Parkway led them into a more exotic and bohemian world than the one they'd known in Scarborough. In 15 or 20 minutes, it took them to the hippest, coolest parts of downtown Toronto.

Years later Myers would vividly remember the

yellow lights along the parkway. To him this was always the yellow brick road that carried him to a fantastic new world, promising wonders that were unheard of in Scarborough.

3

SECOND CITY

W HILE MIKE MYERS WAS IN HIGH SCHOOL in
Scarborough, something remarkable was happening
in downtown Toronto, just a short ride down the
Don Valley Parkway from his home. By the 1970s,
the comedy scene was exploding. Indeed, there were
two distinct schools of comedy, both expanding and
developing, competing with one another for the
loyalty of the new audience—mostly teens and
twenty-somethings who were happily packing grotty-
looking clubs, such as the Old Firehall on Lombard
Street and Yuk Yuk's Komedy Kabaret in Yorkville.

What these clubs were responding to was an appetite for an inexpensive evening of laughter that cut through the blandness and commercialism of TV entertainment.

But these two institutions were not just rivals—they had competing ideologies of comedy, and each had a presiding impresario. The Old Firehall was home to the Toronto branch of Chicago's Second City comedy troupe, which performed sketches featuring social and political satire, and which worshiped at the shrine of improvisation. Toronto had been Second City's second city since 1973, but its early days were so nonlucrative that Bernard Sahlins, Second City's Chicago-based proprietor, sold the Toronto operation to a young hustler named Andrew Alexander for one dollar.

Despite a spectacular lineup of talent—which included John Candy, Eugene Levy, Joe Flaherty, Gilda Radner, Andrea Martin and Catherine O'Hara— the troupe had a hard time drawing audiences until Alexander and Sahlins joined forces to launch a low-budget TV series in the fall of 1976. The series was called *SCTV*, as in Second City Television. And though it started slowly, it turned into such a brilliant and phenomenal success that its cast members became international stars, and the Second City stage show at the Old Firehall became one of Toronto's most beloved and successful entertainment institutions.

What Alexander and Sahlins were reacting to when they launched their TV show was the threat posed by the new late-night comedy program that had begun on NBC in 1975. It featured Mike Myers's favorite older woman, Gilda Radner, who had worked with him on the B.C. hydro commercial. The show was, of course, *Saturday Night Live*, created by another young comedy guru from Toronto, Lorne Michaels. And it succeeded by taking advantage of comedians who had done their apprenticeship with Second City stage companies in Chicago (John Belushi and Bill Murray) and Toronto (Gilda Radner and Dan Aykroyd).

It was obvious to everyone that after years of working for poverty-line wages and playing to tiny audiences, any brilliant young comedian would be eager for the kind of breakthrough that a network TV show could offer—with such striking benefits as exposure to a mass audience and the relatively big paychecks that went with the territory. Sahlins and Alexander were quick to grasp the fact that if they were going to have any hope of hanging on to the talented people performing in their clubs, they would have to provide TV exposure.

In Yorkville, meanwhile, Mark Breslin was squeezing Second City's hold on its market in another way. It was stand-up comedy rather than sketch comedy that interested Breslin. His own sensibility—hip cynicism—

was right in sync with the prevailing aesthetic of the period. And he didn't make the mistake of aiming too high. To Breslin's way of thinking, Second City's brand of revue humor, rooted in academically respectable theater tradition, was too tame. Breslin was flirting with the ruder punk notion that show business stinks. That meant he wasn't afraid to have bad acts as well as good acts. Indeed, razzing the most disastrous performers, and sometimes removing them from the stage with a hook, became one of the cherished traditions at Yuk Yuk's. Audiences loved the idea that the rules of polite society would be dropped, and the shams as well. Nothing was sacred except the art of getting off a good line.

Still, in the late 1970s, several comedians scored breakthrough successes at Yuk Yuk's, including a hard-living iconoclast from Ottawa named Mike MacDonald and a sweet young impressionist from a troubled, homeless family by the name of Jim Carrey.

These were the heady days of comedy in Toronto, when there was not only an edginess but also a sense of danger and thrilling unpredictability that energized both the performers and the audiences. And it would have been surprising if Mike Myers, with the ethos of comedy he had picked up from his father and with his own experience acting in commercials and TV drama, had not yearned to be part of it. It was one thing to see

Gilda Radner on *Saturday Night Live* and dream about working on that show some day. But *SNL* was far, far away, whereas other possibilites were close at hand. All he had to do was get into that old Dodge with some buddies and go downtown to the Old Firehall or Yuk Yuk's to catch the excitement and feel part of what was going on. One of Mike's favorite comedians, John Candy, lived in Toronto and could be seen doing hilarious takeoffs on Orson Welles and Luciano Pavarotti on *SCTV* as well as playing the greatest character he ever created—that party-loving blowhard, Johnny LaRue. And sometimes, you could even see Candy performing live at the Firehall.

Midway through high school, Myers made a decision that indicated he knew what kind of career he was headed for. After going through his local junior high, J.B. Tyrrell, he moved on to the high school next door, Sir John A. Macdonald. But instead of finishing there, he opted instead to transfer to Stephen Leacock High School, which was also in Scarborough but not in Myers's school district.

Leacock had two advantages. It was one of the only schools in the whole Toronto area that offered a course in TV production. And it operated on a semester system, which was appealing to anyone who preferred to take the fast track and graduate from high school as soon as possible.

Howard Gross, who taught TV production to
Myers, remembers that he was terrible at the techni-
cal elements but a genius in front of the camera. He
loved hamming it up for the other kids.

According to Gross, Mike was not a mainstream
student. One thing that struck Gross was how absorbed
Mike was in career aspirations at such an early age.

And in retrospect, Gross could see where the character of Wayne Campbell in *Wayne's World* had come
from. According to Gross, Wayne was a composite of
possibly half a dozen kids in Mike's class. A lot of them
had long hair, played guitar and had leather jackets
with fringes.

While he was still in high school, Myers began the
training that would eventually launch his career at
Second City.

Around 1980, Myers enrolled in a Second City
workshop being taught by Allan Guttman, a theater
school graduate from Montreal who had served as
music director for some shows at the Old Firehall and
then segued into teaching young comedians who had
been hired for an offshoot company called the touring
company. Guttman devised workshops for members
of the touring company, and they were so successful
that Andrew Alexander asked him to teach workshops
that would be open to the public. The response was so
great that the workshop program kept expanding.

"This sounds easy to say in hindsight," Guttman recalls, "but I thought Mike was something special right away. The same thing happened earlier the first time I saw Gilda. Occasionally you spot someone and you just know."

Though Mike was a teenager still in school, he struck Guttman as very disciplined and remarkably well-read. He could talk about philosophy, and he was enthusiastic about the plays of Harold Pinter—so enthusiastic that he wrote something in the Pinter style for a playwriting competition and asked Guttman to critique his work.

One of the reasons Guttman was so impressed with Mike was that he seemed to be a genuine original. He was one of the first persons who seemed to have a real 1980s sensibility. He wasn't just aping what comedians had done in the past. Rather, he was in the vanguard of what was going to happen. His pop-culture references were as much of their time as John Candy's and Joe Flaherty's had been of an earlier period.

To Guttman it seemed clear that Mike Myers belonged in the fruitful tradition of Second City—an extended comedy family with its own credo stretching back to Chicago in the 1950s. It had begun as an outgrowth of the Compass Players and other experimental groups, and then turned into an established academy of social satire with an impressive list of

distinguished alumni, including Alan Arkin, Joan
Rivers, David Steinberg, Paul Mazursky and Valerie
Harper.

Compass took off from a concept founder David
Shepherd borrowed from the *commedia dell'arte* (a
form of theater popular in Renaissance Europe,
mainly Italy). A troupe of actors would travel from
one town to another, giving shows without a written
script. Instead, the actors worked from notes and
ideas, relying on the inspiration of the moment, with
an emphasis on such devices as slapstick, mistaken
identity, disguises, deception and swindles. The actors
would operate within a basic framework but had a
great deal of freedom to improvise.

Among Shepherd's early collaborators were Paul
Sills (who later created Storybook Theater), Shelley
Berman, Barbara Harris and Elaine May. Sills was the
son of Viola Sopin, who ran pioneer theater workshops in Chicago, and was the author of a book called
Improvisation for the Theater. Sills adapted his mother's
ideas to the world of cabaret comedy, and the new
mandate became the creation of hip, socially relevant
satiric sketches using improvisational techniques.
That was the theoretical underpinning of the workshop class Myers was taking from Guttman.

Myers and Guttman developed a special rapport
that continued for years. At one point, Myers came to

Guttman to say, with some embarrassment, that he did not have enough money to continue with the classes. Guttman told Myers to forget about the money, and quietly allowed him to attend the workshops free of charge. Myers wrote Guttman a letter expressing his gratitude for this favor. Today, that letter is framed and hangs on the wall of Guttman's office at the Humber College School of Comedy.

Mike was ambitious, and his talent had a number of dimensions. He enjoyed demonstrating his tap-dancing prowess, and he was eager to become a film director. As well, he had intellectual interests, and he asked Guttman to write a reference letter for his application to York University, which he planned to attend after graduating from high school.

He submitted two essays as part of that application. One was entitled "*The Spy Who Loved Me* and Joseph Campbell's Hero Cycle." The other was about the great French movie director Louis Malle's *Lacombe, Lucien*—the story of a young country boy who collab- orates with the Nazis in wartime rural France. In the essay Myers grappled with the question: Was Lucien innately evil, or was he simply a product of his time?

Guttman wrote the most glowing recommendation he had ever given anyone, but in the end Myers decided not to go to university. On the day of his last high school exam in 1982, he auditioned for Second

City's touring company—and got the job.

John Candy had started the Toronto touring company in 1975. Although it was based on the Chicago touring company, a lot of the time it didn't actually do that much touring. Frequently it would fill in for the main company on a slow night at the Old Firehall or do the late-night improvisations after the regular show was over.

One night at the Firehall when the touring company was filling in for the main company, Myers and Kevin Frank were performing a scene called "Job Interview." Myers was playing the boss conducting the interview, and Frank had the role of a nervous candidate. At one point, Myers was supposed to reach up and flick Frank's nose, but the gesture didn't quite go the way it was supposed to. By accident, Myers stuck his finger up Frank's nose.

"There we were in front of a packed house at the Firehall," Frank recalled years later, "with Mike's finger up my nose. True professionals that we were, we giggled through the entire rest of the scene, our lines barely audible."

Roaring with laughter, the audience loved it.

By 1982, the touring company had started to live up to its name. There was a long stint at Deerhurst, an Ontario summer resort, and also a challenging trip across Western Canada that included a lot of one-nighters. The stops included Regina, Medicine Hat and Moose Jaw; the venues were sometimes arenas and skating rinks. Those on the trip were six performers, a stage manager and a music director. They traveled by bus.

The way the system worked, performers in the touring company did not develop their own material but did versions of sketches developed by members of the mainstage company. Perhaps inevitably, Mike Myers often found himself performing roles originally played by Martin Short.

Linda Kash, a veteran comedy actress and director, was in the touring company with Myers, and, being on the road, they spent a lot of time together. She would advise Mike on his love life. Both Kash and Debra McGrath, another member of the troupe, had a sense of maternal responsibility toward Mike, a scrawny teenager, and they felt it was up to them to make sure he got enough to eat.

Still, there was a certain amount of conflict between Mike and other members of the company because he wasn't considered a textbook ensemble member. According to the gospel of improvisational comedy, members of the group are expected to make their fellow performers look great. But thanks to *SCTV*, people like John Candy and Andrea Martin were becoming stars, and ambitious new talent wanted to go that same route. Right from the start, Mike Myers seemed to stand apart from the pack.

Bruce Hunter, a teacher and director who was also in the touring company, recalls: "Mike was hilarious, and his characters were funny, but he wasn't always the easiest guy to work with. He was what one of my mentors called a shiner—someone who would go off on a riff like a shooting star, but wasn't that interested in interacting with other people in the company.

"Mike was a young guy with stars in his eyes, and I cut him a lot of slack. I remember one occasion when I approached Mike directly and told him I wanted him to make more effort to listen to me when we were on stage together. He didn't want me to bring that up; in fact he told me I should be talking to the stage manager."

When Myers found himself in conflict with the director of a touring company show, he turned to Guttman for help. At the time, and in retrospect, Guttman sided with Myers.

"Second City sometimes had very odd hiring practices, and sometimes there were people in charge who had neither the experience nor the temperament needed for the jobs they were supposed to do. In this particular situation, I think Mike had more savvy than his boss, but Mike was not diplomatic. The result was that the two of them were butting heads, and there were a couple of people who wanted to get rid of Mike."

This was the first case of what would become a continuing theme in the life and career of Mike Myers: friction with fellow performers and creative collaborators that friends and allies of Myers would write off as sheer envy.

The tension was making Myers feel hemmed in, and increasingly he got the feeling it was time to try something completely different and make a fresh start somewhere else.

4

MULLARKEY
AND MYERS

IN MAY 1984, Mike Myers celebrated his 21st birthday and realized that, though he had come of age, he
had never lived anywhere outside Toronto. Going
across Canada with the touring company of Second
City had given him a taste for travel and adventure,
but now he was eager to get a bit further away from
home turf. During his two-year stint with the touring
company, he had broken into the comedy business and
done an apprenticeship with the most revered comedy
institution in North America. But he wanted to
broaden his experience, soak up other comedy tradi-

tions and test himself in what his father, Eric, had always told him was the Valhalla of the comedy world.

Other aspiring comedy performers dreamt of making it in Los Angeles or New York, but for Mike Myers there was only one true shrine, one true testing ground where you could see how you measured up to the greats of comedy history.

Clearly it was time for Mike to go to England for a while and immerse himself in the world of Peter Sellers, *Beyond the Fringe*, *Monty Python*, *Benny Hill*, the *Goon Show*, the *Carry On* movies and even that lowest of all lowbrow British TV comedy shows, *On the Buses*.

And so it came to pass that on Halloween 1984, Mike left Toronto and landed in London. During the descent of the plane at Heathrow Airport, he jokingly boasted: "See down there, that's gonna be Mike's town, Mike's town."

For a time, a Toronto girlfriend named Barbara joined him. They were living in a cramped flat in Shepherd's Bush.

During his first week in London, while walking through the Notting Hill underground station, Mike noticed a poster for the Cambridge Footlights. That was a university comedy organization with a certain resonance, because out of it had emerged one of the most acclaimed comedy groups ever, *Beyond the Fringe*, which starred Jonathan Miller, Dudley Moore, Peter Cook and Alan Bennett.

"I knew they were the top outfit," Myers explained later, "so I went along and introduced myself."

As a result, Myers wound up working for the Cambridge Footlights for several months, mostly in the box office but also doing odd jobs like painting sets. And he got one of his first breaks in a show that was a spinoff of Cambridge Footlights. He also had a short gig at a comedy club in Chiswick, appearing on the same bill as a young unknown named Hugh Grant.

One of the performers appearing in Cambridge Footlights was Neil Mullarkey, who struck up a chatty relationship with the young box-office clerk from Toronto.

"I used to be an actor in Canada," Myers said.

"Oh, really?" said Mullarkey.

Myers then summoned up the courage to ask whether Mullarkey might ever consider working up a comedy act with a partner.

"Oh, sure," said Mullarkey.

The way Myers explained it a few months later to CBC Radio interviewer Vicki Gabereau, things took off from there.

"Neil threw me some scraps, we did a few gigs together, and things just sort of took off. We decided to stay together for a while."

They started with improvisations in Myers's flat, using whatever props came to hand, including sofas and spatulas. The idea was to create stage sketches that seemed like something they might perform at a private party. That gave their act the flavor of a Scarborough rec room.

Mike was impatient to achieve instant assimilation, and he was impatient to conquer what he regarded as his accent problem. He even enrolled for something called a Received Pronunciation Class. But the way Mike would later tell the story, the man who taught the class made him feel he would never, ever be able to get the accent right.

"That did nothing for my confidence," Myers quipped.

Despite its legendary comedy history, England in the early 1980s seemed a bit underdeveloped as compared with North America, where comedy clubs were in an expansionist, creatively explosive period.

In England there were a few big comedy stars, and then there was the fringe, with no middle ground.

To Kim Kinnie, who was running a promising organization called the Comedy Store, Myers seemed like an ordinary young man with an extraordinary talent—and a lot of drive. Myers suggested to Kinnie that the Comedy Store ought to try something called comedy improvisation. It was all the rage, he explained, in Chicago, Toronto, New York and Los Angeles. But no one was doing it in England. Mike explained a bit of the history and ethos of Second City, which believed that improvisation was the sacred ritual out of which great comedy was created.

Myers and Mullarkey joined a few other performers, including Paul Merton, to form a group called the Comedy Store Players. It took a year to get the Players going, but their act helped pave the way for what later became a popular TV show on both sides of the Atlantic, *Whose Line Is It Anyway?*

Mullarkey and Myers worked what was known in London as "the alternative comedy circuit." Myers thought the terminology was bizarre, because it carried the suggestion that the material wasn't really funny.

"Actually," Mike explained, "I was introduced to some of the funniest acts I had ever seen, including Paul Merton, Alexei Sayle and most particularly a man I've never seen since, who used to carve 27 different animals out of a block of ice."

Myers found it far from easy to gain career momentum. "Things peaked around 1977," he explained wistfully in a 1985 radio interview. "As far as I can tell, I arrived here about four years too late. There was a period of excitement over comedy fringe and the punk thing. Now we are at the tail end of that."

As far as Mike was concerned, being on the comedy

circuit in England was a bit like being in a rock-and-roll band. He and Mullarkey might get 15 gigs lined up over a few months, but the most they would get out of any one booking was three nights. And so they were forever on the road with their suitcases full of fake noses and other comedy props.

The venues had names like Cynics and Idealists. There were no great temples of comedy but an endless array of small places. Unless you were on the established comedy circuit—reserved for people like Ben Elton and Julie Walters—you had to subsist at the other extreme. The material was often very good, and the performers were undeniably talented, but the places they had to do their stuff in were almost always scummy.

Still, Myers was soaking up the British atmosphere, getting ideas for future material, becoming more familiar with the cultural roots of his parents and getting a lot of laughs out of British eccentricities.

Daily life was like a series of comedy sketches.

"On a London bus," he told Vicki Gabereau, "a wino came up to us and I said to Neil, 'He's a hell of a guy but he'll never play for the Leafs'. Neil, of course, calls them the Toronto Maple Leaves."

The battle for linguistic one-upmanship between the Canadian dude and his Cambridge partner was a syndrome Myers liked to call "The Empire Strikes Back."

On stage Myers and Mullarkey did a sketch called "On the Town," featuring three members of Canada's Royal Canadian Mounted Police visiting London. Mike played one of the Mounties, Neil played another—and the third was a cardboard cutout. The three Mounties tap danced on top of a doubledecker London bus. Their mission was to deliver a supply of maple syrup to Canada House in Trafalgar Square. Along the way, they encountered a Canadian business-man dressed in a red plaid shirt and cap; they got into a fight with Beefeaters in a Soho bar; and they searched for a "Limey dame" to take home as a souvenir.

A short home movie screened as part of their show starred a plastic peeing toy known as "Mr. Big."

Myers also introduced a character called Dr. Wicked, using a mask made out of a dish towel and black-rimmed glasses.

As a team, Myers and Mullarkey had something unique—a transatlantic chemistry that made a hugely favorable impression on British reviewers.

"Hilarious ability to create an entire world of sound and objects," said London's *Time Out* entertainment guide. "They inject more into an hour than lesser double acts manage to leak into two or three," said *Stop Press* in Cambridge. And *Lam* magazine declared: "This comedy duo shines out as being among the cleverest, most inspired new acts to have emerged in a long, long time."

After working the circuit for almost a year, Myers went to Edinburgh to participate in the Festival Fringe, picking up a few bookings in church halls for token wages. In Edinburgh, Myers was one of six people sharing a flat, along with Kinnie, Mullarkey, Merton and other members of the Comedy Store Players. Various other people would turn up in the middle of the night. On some nights, Myers seemed like a party animal; but if he was due to perform the next day, he turned into a much more serious and subdued character.

Karen Koren, who ran a Fringe comedy club called the Gilded Balloon, remembers Myers as friendly and committed. But one image sticks in her mind: Mike in his dressing room, sweating profusely from his physically exhausting performance, wearing nothing but his blue Y-front briefs.

One of his flatmates recalled that Myers was hard up for cash at the time, but he never stole anyone's cornflakes, and he always bought his round of drinks.

After serving their apprenticeship in grotty clubs and the upstairs rooms of pubs, Mullarkey and Myers landed a regular spot on a well-known morning children's program called the *Wide Awake Club*, hosted by Timmy Mallett.

The show was produced, directed and edited for
Britain's commercial ITV network by Nick Wilson,
who recalled that Myers and Mullarkey worked for
such low wages that they might have done better on
welfare. Both of them took advantage of the chance to
scoff free breakfasts at ITV's canteen.

Well, considering that the show was produced live
at 7:30 in the morning, where else could they go for
breakfast? They finished work so early the pubs
weren't open yet.

According to Wilson, the humor of the *Wide Awake
Club* was similar to adult humor, only with the
naughty bits edited out. Myers and Mullarkey used
their segment to poke fun at the rest of the show.

"We'd have bedhead hair and robes and were all
grumpy in that haven't-had-your-morning-coffee-yet
kind of way," Mike recalled years later. "I absolutely
loved it, and I think there was a lot of funny stuff on
that show."

Much of the time, their act went over the heads of
the program's young viewers. Occasionally, Myers had
an attack of stage fright, but more often than not the
two seemed to be having a wonderful time and bliss-
ing out on true teamwork.

Their routine was called the "Sound Asleep Club."
Myers and Mullarkey would wander on screen in their
pajamas, clutching teddy bears and pretending to be

half asleep.

It was unlike conventional children's TV fare in England at that time, and it was considered cutting-edge and revolutionary.

Mike was hardly an established star, but he was beginning to make his way in England, and he felt that his decision to go there had been a good one. Had he headed for Los Angeles, he would have been trapped in the usual catch-22 situation of young performers: If you haven't worked, you can't get an agent; but if you don't have an agent, you can't get work.

Mike was especially keen to get film work, and he spotted an ad in a daily casting sheet that he and his actor friends pooled their resources to buy. "Young Americans wanted," the ad said. The film in question was Stanley Kubrick's *Full Metal Jacket*. Having no agent, Myers called the film's casting director himself—and got an appointment.

For his screen test, Myers chose to read a monologue from the play *Kennedy's Children*. The casting director said it was great and promised to send it right to Kubrick.

Then one day the communal pay phone rang, and it was for Mike. At the other end of the phone was a man with a thick Australian accent who said he was from Kubrick's office.

"Stanley loved the tape," said the Australian man.

"He wants you to come in for a callback."

Mike, who was down to his last $10 at the time, was so thrilled he sat down and cried.

In the end, though, he didn't get the part in *Full Metal Jacket*.

However, Kubrick's office recommended him for other parts, which is why he turned up playing a delivery guy in *John and Yoko: A Love Story*.

By then, Mike did have an agent. "He's a nice modest agent, but he has the desire to become a hotshot," he told Vicki Gabereau. "He wants to make a lot of money, which I think is nice."

Yet he was homesick for Toronto. He had relatives in England but they all lived in Liverpool, so he rarely saw them. He couldn't follow the Maple Leafs, except for special occasions, such as Stanley Cup playoff games—at least one of which he watched at Canada House in Trafalgar Square, while consuming as much beer as possible.

Mike liked to make jokes in which England was unfavorably compared with Canada. British electrical outlets were ludicrously large, in his view; and though they'd survived the Blitz and won World War II, the English had failed to master the art of mixing hot water with cold water and having it come out of one tap.

Mike was missing a lot of things about home, including Scarborough doughnut shops and Canadian summers.

Then came word from Toronto that Eric Myers, Mike's beloved father, was in failing health.

It was time to move back to the other side of the Atlantic.

5

It's Only Rock 'n' Roll

For mike myers, almost two years in England had been an excellent adventure and a kind of apprenticeship in a comedy kingdom that had been mythologized throughout his childhood. Being there and working there had been a meaningful rite of passage. But coming home to Toronto in the summer of 1986 was a pleasure and a great liberation for Mike. Much as he treasured British eccentricity, he had never quite felt at home in England. He longed for his parents and brothers, *Late Night with David Letterman*, the Toronto Maple Leafs and Doritos.

Mike had also missed playing to audiences who would instantly understand his cultural frame of reference without having the jokes explained. There was no point presenting a character like Wayne Campbell, the Scarborough teenager, for British audiences, because they'd have to take a course in Canadian suburban sociology before being able to comprehend just what was being satirized. But in Toronto, Mike could relax and slip into his characters without the burden of worrying about all that. And he did.

For starters, Mike enjoyed the triumph of being invited to perform on the mainstage of Second City, at the Old Firehall in downtown Toronto, where he used to go as a Scarborough teen to see John Candy, Eugene Levy, Dave Thomas, Martin Short, Andrea Martin and Catherine O'Hara. In those days, he had been a teen escaping Scarberian blight through the magic of the Don Valley Parkway. But this time around, he was living right downtown, over a Korean fruit store near Honest Ed's emporium in the Bathurst and Bloor area. And Mike, who had turned 23 in May and seemed strikingly young even by the standards of the comedy world, felt honored to be courted by the management of Second City.

By the mid-1980s, the Toronto branch of Second City was suffering a bit of a midlife crisis. Its brilliant first generation of stars had gone on to Hollywood

careers. Its inspired spinoff TV show, *SCTV*, had
finally left the air after seven tumultous years. And the
whole enterprise was getting a little too predictable, a
little too comfortable. Even the audience was getting
a bit older and more conventional. The critics,
inevitably, kept referring to the formula involved in
concocting a Second City show.

In April 1986—a few months before Mike returned
from England—the Toronto branch of Second City
opened its 24th cabaret revue at the Old Firehall on
Lombard Street. The show was called *Bordering on
Madness*, or *Who's Tory Now?* and it boasted what was
billed as an excitingly fresh new cast. Many of them
were recruited from the national touring cast or the
cast at Second City's new club in London, Ontario.

Most of the big laughs in the show were generated by
the only two women in the cast of six, Deborah Theaker
and Linda Kash. One of the high points of the show was
a Shakespeare spoof in which Kash and Theaker played
boys who were actually girls pretending to be boys, and
got to deliver nonsensical lines, such as "Who goes
there? . . . Be it Tudor, son of Four-door and Coupe?"
Kash and Theaker were also outstanding in another
sketch about a born-again couple who had found "the
power of righteous living." And they had great fun
playing a couple of celebrated Canadian folksingers
named Buffy St. Elsewhere and Joni Bitchin.

But the four men in the show—Mark Wilson, David Huband, Bob Bainborough and Dana Andersen—had a rougher time, with the possible exception of Andersen. Although Kash earned a nomination for a Dora Mavor Moore Award, *Bordering on Madness* drew mixed reviews punctuated by faint praise and a lot of reservations.

"They're still a little green," wrote Rob Salem in the *Toronto Star*.

"By Second City standards, this show is a cut below what it should be," was the verdict of Ray Conlogue in the *Globe and Mail*.

Obviously, an infusion of dazzling new talent was needed—especially a guy who could be embraced as the next John Candy or the next Martin Short. And so an availability check went to Mike in England.

As things turned out, Mike was exactly what Second City needed. Young, ambitious and energetic, he was at the point where everything was coming together. And he was psyched up about the opportunity of making it in on Second City's mainstage.

Once Mike was back on Toronto soil, he felt very much at home. He understood, in a way he never could in England, who was in the audience, where they were coming from and how they'd grown up. And perhaps for the first time, he had enough experience that he didn't have to feel insecure and defensive the way he often had in the past.

In mid-November, Myers helped Second City achieve one of its biggest hits of the decade—a witty, eclectic revue entitled *Not Based on Anything by Stephen King*, briskly directed by John Hemphill. The targets of the satirical humor ranged from doctors addicted to extra-billing, to a Toronto bus driver who thinks he's a priest, to aspiring politicians and consumers too stupid to notice the difference between a telephone and an iron. Among the cultural and political references: Emily Brontë, who comes on as a stand-up comedienne, and Karl Marx, whose life story is turned into an Irving Berlin musical featuring such songs as "A Pretty Girl Is Like a Commodity."

Once again Linda Kash and Deborah Theaker were standout performers. But this time, the men (Myers, Bainborough, Andersen, Wilson, Bruce Pirrie and music director Bob Derkach) were notably stronger than in the previous show. The *Globe and Mail* noted that the frantic innocence of Mike Myers had become "a touchstone" for the company.

Still, Mike Myers didn't play the improv game quite the way the orthodox rules stipulated. As Kash put it somewhat diplomatically: "Some performers are just different. They are solo acts within the company. Maybe it's not the way an ensemble is supposed to be, but they have the drive and the incentive to stick out, and the best way to work with them is just to let them take the lead and marvel at what they can do."

And what Mike could do was create wild and crazy characters for himself—even if he didn't seem all that interested in setting up comic opportunities for his colleagues. Two of the characters Mike developed at the Old Firehall were destined to become phenomenally popular with audiences well beyond Toronto. First there was a character Mike had been working on since he was 12—Wayne Campbell, a Scarborough teenager with a fondness for heavy metal, doughnut shops and phrases like "We're not worthy" and "No way! . . . Way!"

And then there was Dieter, an avant-garde, über-serious German talk-show host, whose most famous line was "Touch my monkey."

Just who contributed what to the creation of these characters would become increasingly controversial in the years to come.

Soon after he began performing regularly at the Old Firehall, Mike attracted the attention of a team of TV producers who were seeking fresh comedy talent for a hip new TV variety series. The half-hour show, called *It's Only Rock 'n' Roll,* was produced by John Brunton's Insight Productions for the CBC, and it featured a combination of rock music and the kind of comedy that would appeal to people who follow rock music.

Brunton conceived the show in collaboration with Joe Bodolai, a writer-producer who had a track record writing *Saturday Night Live*. They felt the CBC was the perfect place to do the kind of show they had in mind, especially since Ivan Fecan, then the CBC's director of network programming, was eager to develop younger audiences.

The show was taped at CBC Toronto's Studio Seven, which reeked of history. This was the studio where the celebrated comedy team Wayne and Shuster did their sketches. It was the studio where Norman Jewison had started his directing career back in the 1950s.

The hosts of the show—chosen by John Brunton, Joe Bodolai and co-producer Judith Dryland—were Ted Woloshyn, a quick-witted veteran radio host, and Fred Mollin, later known as composer of music for the TV series *Forever Knight*.

The producers were all fans of Second City, and they went to the Old Firehall hoping to find talent that could make the jump to TV. They were not disappointed. Among their discoveries was Linda Kash, who performed a Singing Nun spoof written by Bodolai—to considerable acclaim.

The show turned out to be a frantic, eclectic half-hour mixing bits of rock music (with performances by such bands as Blue Rodeo) and comedy skits. It seemed to incorporate bits and pieces of familiar, established shows, including *Much Music, Late Night with David Letterman* and *Entertainment Tonight*. There were regular appearances by a number of performers, including Fred Mollin, Shawn Thompson, Dan Gallagher and Taborah Johnson.

The show was designed to appeal to a young audience, but the CBC traditionally appealed to a broader and older audience. The edgier the show became, the narrower its appeal. The program went through a kind of shakedown period, finding its way, and jumping, at the end of August, after two months on the air, from its 8 P.M. time slot to an 11:30 P.M. late-night slot on Fridays—a slot, ironically, occupied several years earlier by *SCTV*.

As Brunton acknowledges, *It's Only Rock 'n' Roll* was very much a work in progess. On the way to reaching the air, there was a kind of spring training session during which everyone involved got to try out ideas. And right from the start, the program was up against some daunting scheduling oddities. First, it began life in June, just as many regular viewers were tuning out for the summer. And the slot it was originally given, 8 P.M. on Fridays, meant it was on too early to be really edgy, really raunchy or really daring.

Mike had already appeared as Scarborough teenage Wayne Campbell on Citytv, a local Toronto channel, but *It's Only Rock 'n' Roll* turned out to be a perfect vehicle for bringing him to a larger audience along with two of his most inspired characters—Wayne Campbell and the weird German aesthete named Dieter.

A few months before the show went into production, Brunton and his team of producers and writers made regular forays to the Old Firehall to watch Second City performances. They were trying to figure out who were the brightest and best comedy talents available. Mike Myers stood out.

It wasn't until halfway through the season that Myers began showing up week after week on *It's Only Rock 'n' Roll*. In retrospect, you can't help wondering whether the program would have lasted more than one season if Myers had been involved from the beginning and had been given a more central role.

According to Brunton, once Mike was chosen for the show, he was so eager to succeed that he would arrive for work every morning pitching ideas. Of all the performers connected with the program, he was the one who showed the most get-up-and-go, in Brunton's recollection.

"Mike was a man on a mission," Brunton recalls. "He was an emerging star, having been in showbiz since he was a kid, and everyone could sense it."

Midway through the season, the audience was told

there had been a contest for a regular guest spot on the show. The winner was a guy from Scarborough named Wayne Campbell, who henceforth turned up weekly with a mini-feature called "Wayne's Power Minute."

In one episode, Wayne complained that there's something wrong when people discuss the three R's of education, because really only one of those words actually starts with an R. "Who's to blame?" he asks. "Well, frankly, I blame society."

On another occasion, Wayne explained just how he'd won the contest. He was required to write in and explain in 10 words what he thought of the show. "So I wrote in and said 'Excellent.' So I won."

Occasionally, Wayne got a little obsessive. One of his power minutes was devoted to handshakes. Wayne claimed there are just too many different kinds of handshakes in the world, leaving people paralyzed with indecision. Another thing that bugged Wayne: the use of the word "party" as a verb.

Wayne also emerged as a bit of a social crusader. He had a camper ambulance, which he used to do charity work. The chief benefactors: people who suffer from being partied out.

"Chicks come to me and say 'My boyfriend grossed me out.' I talk them out of it."

In Wayne's view, this is a public service that should

really be paid for by the government.

He wondered why it wasn't.

"I blame society," says Wayne.

After the last episode of *It's Only Rock 'n' Roll* was taped, Brunton had a big party at his house in the Leaside area of Toronto. The party had a Mexican theme, so the guests were drinking tequila and margaritas, and the party turned out to be a raucous enough affair to draw a visit from the police.

Myers and his Second City cohorts arrived late, because they had given a performance that night at the Old Firehall.

"Mike and Dana arrived together and since it was late they had a lot of catching up to do," Brunton recalls.

They started performing in the family room of Brunton's house. First, Myers would do a comedy bit, and then Andersen would try to top it. It turned into the kind of competition that inspired Irving Berlin's song "Anything You Can Do I Can Do Better."

The two of them were magnificently funny, competing with one another for laughs, and the other guests knew they were witnessing something special.

At the time, no one realized that one of these two guys would remain a fairly obscure performer, and the other would become one of the world's biggest stars. And it wouldn't have occurred to anyone that the friendship of these two cutups would be severely strained over the years, with Andersen publicly chastising Myers for failing to acknowledge Andersen's contribution after Dieter became a huge hit on *Saturday Night Live.*

That night, few people foresaw that the giddy roller-coaster ride of putting *It's Only Rock 'n' Roll* on the air would end in bitterness and disappointment. And one of the things that would rankle its creators was that, as far as most of the world was concerned, it was *Saturday Night Live* and Lorne Michaels who would get credit for putting Mike Myers on TV playing Wayne Campbell and Dieter—when in fact these characters made their TV debuts on *It's Only Rock 'n' Roll.*

Why did the show expire after only one short season? Well, the newspaper reviews had been mixed, and the CBC was a bit perplexed and unsure of what to do with a program that seemed to be constantly reinventing itself. Initially, music had been the most important component, and comedy was strictly incidental. But as the show evolved, comedy became even more important than music.

By the end of September 1987, all 13 shows of the first season had run, and the CBC was wavering about the show's future.

"We were holding on, and there was a certain

amount of burnout," says Brunton. "We were asked to do a New Year's Eve special, and we were frustrated that's all we were asked to do. People felt as if they had been pushing a big rock up a steep hill. A lot of people involved in doing the show were tremendously ambitious.

"They felt this had been a great experience, but it was enough. The gang collectively elected not to do the New Year's show. When we gave the CBC our answer, that was effectively the end of *It's Only Rock 'n' Roll*."

Still, the CBC kept the public's memory of the series alive by presenting an hour-long Christmas show that consisted of highlights from earlier episodes. And a year after *It's Only Rock 'n' Roll* ceased production, Brunton, Bodolai and Dryland won a Gemini award for producing the best variety show on Canadian television.

In retrospect, it would be remembered as a curiosity, and a blip in CBC programming. But if it had lasted a bit longer and been seen by more viewers, *It's Only Rock 'n' Roll* would have had a place of honor in TV history as the show that brought Wayne Campbell and Dieter to a network television audience.

6

CHICAGO

IN LATE JUNE 1987, Mike Myers and the rest of the cast from *Not Based on Anything by Stephen King* scored an odd triumph when collectively they won the Dora Mavor Moore Award for creating the best original musical or revue of the season. The only problem was they had the sole nomination in their category, since evidently there had not been any other original musical or comedy worth nominating in Toronto theater that year. Consequently, the award was clouded by controversy about whether it should have been given at all.

Two nights after the Dora Awards, Mike had
another opening, another show at the Old Firehall. As
things turned out, the Toronto company's 26th show,
Bob Has Seen the Wind, would mark Mike's last
opening at the old Second City club on Lombard
Street. And after the memorable high spots of *Not
Based on Anything by Stephen King*, there was perhaps
inevitably a sense of letdown about *Bob Has Seen the
Wind*.

"First-rate stuff is not all that common in the new
show, although it does have its moments," wrote Ray
Conlogue in the *Globe and Mail*. "It was almost as if
the churning energy and excellence of *Not Based on
Anything by Stephen King* had exhausted the cast. All
those clever topical digs and complicated, elegant
ideas just kind of wore everybody out, it seems."

Christopher Hume in the *Toronto Star* was more
forgiving. According to Hume, Myers and the other
five members of the cast—Dana Andersen, Ryan
Stiles, Deborah Theaker, Audrey Webb and Mark
Wilson—performed in appropriately manic fashion.

"Even when the skits aren't funny," wrote Hume,
"their lunatic antics pull them through."

A few members of the previous fall's Dora-winning
ensemble had moved on, but *Bob Has Seen the Wind*
did introduce one comedy star of the future, Ryan
Stiles. Stiles was a tall, rangy American who had come

to the Old Firehall by way of Vancouver and would soon become best known to Second City patrons for his memorable impression of Gorbachev, and to TV viewers for his success, along with fellow Second City performer Colin Mochrie, on the TV game show *Whose Line Is It Anyway?* Later still, he became a regular on a popular U.S. network sitcom, the *Drew Carey Show*.

But for a lot of people, *Bob Has Seen the Wind* was worth seeing for the hilarious performance of Mike Myers in the unlikely role of Anne of Green Gables.

The premise of the spoof: What if the film version of the beloved Charlottetown Festival musical based on Lucy Maud Montgomery's classic were to be directed by David Cronenberg, Toronto's master of perversity?

And so on came Mike Myers as a hairy-legged little orphan, singing her signature song in a basso profundo voice with an echo effect. This particular Anne also managed to blind the local minister while forcing his wife into childbirth, and to rip out her friend Gilbert's lungs.

In December 1987, Mike got a chance to perform some of his Second City material for a huge TV audience across North America. *SCTV* had been off the air for several years, and Andrew Alexander was determined to get a new Second City show on the air, especially in the U.S. market. He had even gone so far as to open a new Second City club in Santa Monica, California, so that he could more easily attract attention from TV network scouts—bringing in performers from Chicago and Toronto, and show-casing sitcom ideas live on stage, right in front of the L.A. network TV people.

That's how he got CBS involved in a show called *110 Lombard*—an hour-long hybrid, part sketch comedy, part sitcom—whose title referred to the address of the Old Firehall in downtown Toronto. Once the deal was made with CBS, Atlantis Productions produced a pilot episode in Toronto.

The story concerns the relationship of three single guys—played by Myers, Bob Bainborough and Ryan Stiles—who share a low-rent downtown loft. Amid much male bonding, the three dudes confront such threats to their collective security as impotence and marriage-minded women. But the storyline is just an excuse for the performers to show off their comedy prowess, with much of the material parachuted in from Second City stage skits.

Supporting players included such other talented Second City performers as Linda Kash, Bonnie Hunt, Don Lake, Bruce Pirrie and Dana Andersen. And the first episode also featured a musical interlude to break up the comedy.

Richard Kind—a clown who had become known in Chicago for playing loud-mouthed, intrusive characters—brought a sketch he had developed at the Second City club in Chicago. It was about a wealthy man whose philosophy of life was "Never fuck a kidder." Mike Myers played the extremely unqualified suitor of the rich guy's daughter.

CBS was looking for a replacement for a dreadful program called *Top of the Pops* in its late-night Friday slot. The CBC was very interested in being a partner broadcaster as well.

Unfortunately, Alexander was not able to get CBS to go for a series. Instead the network gave the late-night Friday slot to Pat Sajak.

Mike spent most nights of 1987 performing at the Firehall, but a lot of the time, he didn't feel much like laughing. Eric, who was not only Mike's father but also his comedy guru and the inspiration for just about everything Mike had ever done, had been diagnosed with Alzheimer's. Eric's personality seemed to be unraveling right in front of his family, much to Mike's horror and dismay.

The diagnosis had confirmed what had become increasingly apparent to Mike: Something was very wrong. Eric had already confided to Mike that he was scared because he knew he was forgetting things, and Mike had picked up the unnerving early signs that

Eric was getting increasingly confused about various details of daily life.

"I felt I'd been hit in the chest with a pile driver," Mike later told *People* magazine. "It was one of the bleakest periods of my life."

Still, 1987 was also the year when something wonderful happened to Mike. While he was on a trip to Chicago to catch a hockey game between the Maple Leafs and the Chicago Blackhawks, he met an aspiring young actor/writer named Robin Ruzan, and fell in love with her.

Her background could hardly have been more different from his. Born and raised in the Queens section of New York City, Robin came from a warm, cheerfully chaotic Jewish household, where speaking your mind bluntly and forcefully was a way of life.

To Robin, Mike was an exotic creature—being Canadian, suburban and Gentile. According to Joyce Sloane, who was running Second City's Chicago operation, Mike fell immediately in love with Robin and made it clear he had to be with her.

Looking back on it later, Myers mused: "What shocked us both was how different our upbringings were but how we nevertheless came to the same conclusions about how we wanted to live. We literally do say 'How did we find each other? What are the odds? I mean I'm so Protestant, so English and so

Canadian. She's Jewish, such a New Yorker and so American. I don't even know if it's a case of opposites attracting each other. It's more like two different laboratories came up with the same equation."

Mike thought of Robin as his muse. She could be brutally critical of his sketches, and he came to rely on her judgment. She would often tell him that he talked too much. She liked to concentrate on sunsets, babies and dogs in silence. "It's not a verbal experience right now," she would tell Mike when she wanted him to stop talking.

The way things turned out, Chicago was the city where they could try living together.

Mike had some qualms about moving there, but Second City owner Andrew Alexander asked him to go, and Myers realized it was a special opportunity. Much as he enjoyed working with Toronto's Second City company, the Chicago company had a longer, richer history that few Toronto performers got a chance to tap into.

One who had was John Candy, one of Mike's idols, who had done an apprenticeship 15 years earlier. Candy had been lucky enough to have one of Second City's other cast members, a young guy named Bill Murray, to show him the town.

Joyce Sloane, one of the original Second City pioneers, had helped Candy make his way in Chicago, and she was still there when Mike arrived.

But there was a snag. As a Canadian, Mike required a green card to work in Chicago. And it took a couple of months before the green card came through. Luckily, the delay gave him a prized opportunity. While he was waiting for his green card, Mike was invited to take classes with Chicago's revered and lovably eccentric improv guru, Del Close, who had been a mentor to John Belushi, Bill Murray and Shelley Long.

Though he had an honored place in the history of Second City, Close had an even stronger association with the newer and more experimental ImprovOlympic, which was co-founded by Charna Halpern and David Shepherd in 1981. (A year later Close had replaced Shepherd as Halpern's partner.) To the public, this comedy laboratory on Clark Street near Wrigley Field was not nearly as well-known as Second City. Yet within the business, Second City was considered a magnet for tourists, whereas ImprovOlympic was regarded as excitingly innovative.

It was here that Close created his revolutionary long-form improv technique, known as the Harold. During a 45–minute session, performers would develop and return to themes. Inevitably ImprovOlympic became a kind of farm team for Second City; it was understood in the business that if you wanted to perform on the mainstage at Second City, the way to get there was to train at ImprovOlympic.

Sometimes Andrew Alexander would arrange for Close and Halpern to do workshops with Second City players, and in 1987, Alexander brought the pair to Toronto to do a workshop with the cast at the Old Firehall. That's how Mike Myers became a protegé of Del Close (who died in 1999, and whose skull rests at the Goodman Theatre, awaiting a chance to play Yorick in *Hamlet*, as decreed in Close's will).

"Mike was mesmerized by Del and just loved him," Halpern recalls. "I think it was one of the reasons he agreed to come to Chicago. He learned how to work creatively within an ensemble. At Second City, you could be a star, but at our place you were just one of eight players, and everyone had to connect with everyone else. Mike loved the things we showed him. He latched onto details he could invent, like scenery, costumes, choreography, posters and the small physical elements of a scene."

What dazzled Myers about Close was his intuitive approach combined with his intellect. His gift for synthesizing reminded Mike of Joseph Campbell, who could examine different hero myths and distill them into geometric shapes as a way of explaining how they were alike in some ways and different in others.

In the introduction to Halpern's book *Truth in Comedy*, Myers wrote: "The Harold is an improv game that blew me away and continues to blow me away. It isn't just a game; it's a way of looking at life. The basic principle is adaptation, and being adaptive is the most crucial lesson I've learned. It provides you with a glossary of terms for the creative process and identifies recurring patterns in your imagination. It's the Zen approach to comedy. Most important, it's a lot of fun. Whenever I'm blocked, I return to the methods of the Harold. After all, the end is in the beginning."

Once his green card came through, Mike wound up at Second City working on a show called *Kuwait Until Dark*, or *Bright Lights, Night Baseball*. But he returned to ImprovOlympic on Monday nights, when Second City was dark, and any other chance he got.

Kuwait was being directed by Betty Thomas, who had been wooed back to the Second City club on North Wells Street in Chicago's Old Town, where she had started as a waitress in the early 1970s and then gone on to become a performer alongside John Candy and Bill Murray.

Betty was known as a bit of a wild woman and a tomboy, famous for not wearing underwear and for driving a truck long before it was fashionable for women to do so. After leaving Second City, she had moved to Los Angeles. When he learned that Thomas had become a successful TV director on the Emmy Award winning NBC police series *Hill Street Blues*, Alexander decided it would be a great idea to bring her back to Chicago to direct a Second City show.

There weren't that many people who had the knack of directing Second City revues. And that meant Alexander had a problem when Bernard Sahlins decided in 1988, after 30 years, that he no longer wanted to direct.

By that time, Sahlins felt he could no longer understand the audience and had no one left to talk to. The first generation of Second City performers and audiences had a pre-TV sensibility; that is, they had a literary/intellectual background; most of them were associated with the University of Chicago, and their childhoods had not been shaped by TV. Then came a generation who were children of the TV age, but who still took an intellectual approach to it. By the late 1980s, however, Sahlins was encountering people whose entire frame of reference was TV—and he felt as if they had come from another planet.

Besides, the management of Second City constantly had to confront the complaint that the troupe's material was too tame, too formulaic, too much like a slight recap of what had seemed fresher and funnier in an earlier incarnation of the venerable comedy institution. Joyce Sloane had to cope with the worst insult of

all—the contemptuous view of Second City's harshest
critics that, after 30 years and almost 70 productions,
the club was so tired and feeble it had become a tourist
trap.

Betty Thomas and Mike Myers were among the
people brought in to give the proceedings a much-
needed zap. And in *Kuwait Until Dark*, which opened
in June 1988, Thomas proved she knew exactly how to
put together a smooth-running show.

The cast featured five men and two women. Besides
Mike Myers, the men were Steve Assad, Kevin Crowley,
Aaron Freeman and Joe Liss. The two women, Bonnie
Hunt and Barbara Wallace, were praised by reviewers as
being among the sharpest performers.

In the show's first scene, two archaeologists from a
National Geographic special about the future opened an
entombed cabaret and speculated about the strange
rituals that might have gone on there in the past. It
was a witty way to position *Kuwait Until Dark* as a
satiric time capsule about life in 1988, when people
seemed to be concerned with such matters as
Panamanian politics, the cancellation of smoking priv-
ileges on commercial airlines, the pursuit of safe sex
and unsafe drugs, the absurd process of choosing U.S.
presidential candidates, and the apparent collapse of
family life, organized religion and the Chicago public
school system.

According to Heidi Weiss, who reviewed the show for the *Sun-Times,* until intermission, *Kuwait Until Dark* seemed disappointing and lightweight, just as most Second City productions had been in recent years. But during the second half, she noticed a welcome change. Several sketches were biting, and one was almost dangerous.

Among the better sketches was one called "Saskafarian," in which Myers took up a theme suggested by someone in the audience, education, and went on to create a reggae song, mocking the pseudo-revolutionary quality of reggae lyrics.

And what about the sketch that reached the giddy heights of being almost dangerous?

Well, it was a takeoff on the popular PBS public-affairs show *Firing Line,* with ultraconservative host William F. Buckley. In the Second City version, Steve Assad did a clever impression of Buckley. His guests included a spokesman from an African country (played by Aaron Freeman) and a dropout from the Chicago school system (Mike Myers) who has made a fortune by selling Dove Bars and hawking T-shirts.

The dangerous part came when the conversation turned to the delicate question of whether the black cultural influence of rock 'n' roll might be partly responsible for the educational crisis looming throughout the United States.

Despite his apparent success on stage, for Myers, adjusting to the difference between Toronto and Chicago was not easy. The Chicago group was incestuous and close-knit, and Myers was regarded by some as an outsider and a carpetbagger. Members of the Chicago touring company felt this intruder from a foreign country had jumped the queue when rightly one of them should have had a chance to take the vacant spot in the mainstage company.

As a social satirist, Mike was struck by some amusing cultural differences between Canada and the United States. One was the speediness with which you could get a new bed.

He and Robin had decided to move in together really quickly. They urgently needed a new bed. Robin found a place that agreed to deliver a bed within an hour. Meanwhile, they decided to order ribs from the Fireplace.

The way Mike told the story years later, the mattress beat the ribs.

"We set it up, the food came, and we ate it on the mattress and watched TV. And I thought, 'God bless America.'"

In August 1988, while *Kuwait Until Dark* was running, Myers asked Sloane for a night off. He wanted to go home for a special show celebrating the 15th anniversary of the Toronto club.

Sloane consented. As a result, everything was about to change for Mike.

7

LIVE FROM NEW YORK

IT WAS THE KIND OF NIGHT people talk about for
years—and one of the turning points in the life of
Mike Myers. It happened on a Sunday in late August
1988 at the Old Firehall. Point of the exercise: a star-
studded blowout to celebrate 15 years of Second City
in Toronto.

The Firehall holds only 300 people, so this one-
time only dinner show/birthday bash was one of the
hottest comedy tickets of the decade.

Among those present were many of the people
who had made the place one of Toronto's beloved

entertainment spots: Andrew Alexander, Sally Cochrane, Joe Flaherty, Dave Thomas, Catherine O'Hara, Andrea Martin, Martin Short, Robin Duke, Valri Bromfield, Eugene Levy, Rosemary Radcliffe, Jayne Eastwood, Ben Gordon, John Hemphill, Don Lake, Ron James, Debra McGrath, Bruce Pirrie, Sandra Balcovske, Linda Kash, Deborah Theaker; and from Chicago: Bernie Sahlins, Joyce Sloane, Del Close and Charna Halpern.

A special celebrity guest was also there: Michael Keaton, star of that summer's hit movie *Beetlejuice*, who was in town shooting his next movie, *Dream Team*.

There wasn't space for a green room; instead, a green tent had been set up in the parking lot, where VIP guests and performers could mill about.

Some party-goers stayed until dawn on Monday.

Conspicuously absent were John Candy (still feuding with Alexander at the time) and Dan Aykroyd.

The marathon evening began with cocktails at five o'clock. Catherine O'Hara provided special volunteer services—doing makeup and hair for various people. The festivities carried right on through four hours of comedy sketches (taped and edited into a one-hour TV special), followed by a buffet dinner.

In retrospect, there's one thing almost everyone can agree on: Mike Myers stole the show, especially when

he was teamed with Martin Short, playing a Second
City improv game called "Freeze Tag."

"He was just so hysterically funny people wanted it
to go on forever," Halpern recalls.

A number of people said Myers was the next Martin
Short.

"Who is that guy?" Michael Keaton asked Charna
Halpern.

Suddenly, Lorne Michaels—the former Torontonian
who had changed TV history by creating *Saturday
Night Live* in 1975—was getting a lot of calls. He heard
from agent Pam Thomas, then married to Dave
Thomas. He heard from Michael Keaton. And he heard
from Martin Short.

"You've got to hire this guy," they all said.

Two weeks after the anniversary show, Myers got a
phone call from *Saturday Night Live*. Lorne Michaels
wanted to arrange a meeting. Soon afterward, Myers
flew to New York for an audition.

He was hired as a writer and feature player, and he
made his *Saturday Night Live* debut as a featured
performer in January 1989.

The first sketch he wrote was called "Mock Me."
The most memorable line of dialogue was: "You mock
me, and I will not be mocked!"

Mike wrote the sketch with Al Franken. He wrote
a small part for himself. Later, he decided that had

been a foolish move; he should have written himself a big part.

It didn't take him long to learn.

At the time Myers joined the show, *Saturday Night Live* was on the rebound, going into one of its richest periods after many years of decline. And it was drawing an audience of about 12 million viewers every week.

For years, critics were in the habit of looking back to its glory days in the late 1970s, when Lorne Michaels, then a young wizard from CBC Toronto, had created something truly revolutionary—a weekly late-night comedy show that combined the latest in pop music with the kind of sharp, satirical comedy sketches considered too daring for prime-time network TV.

Saturday Night Live delivered to NBC a large, hip audience that was otherwise less responsive to network TV fare—especially such square early 1970s programs as *Marcus Welby, MD.* Those who considered themselves too funky and smart for prime time tended to be extremely receptive to the fresh, funny new faces emerging from obscure comedy clubs across North America. Consequently, it was through *Saturday Night Live* that Bill Murray, Eddie Murphy, John Belushi and Chevy Chase began their ascent to movie stardom.

Miraculously, *Saturday Night Live* seemed able to

restore the energy and excitement of TV's early days, being performed before a live audience. But after just a few seasons, the thrill seemed to be gone. The show was in a way a victim of its own success; it became so hot so fast that its most popular performers got better offers, and many left to pursue Hollywood movie careers. Meanwhile other programs came along to compete—including *SCTV*, which began as a tiny, low-budget series in Canada but found its way into U.S. syndication and landed for a time on NBC.

Lorne Michaels, declared a genius only a few years earlier, was by the late 1970s said to have lost his edge, and already people were remarking wistfully that *SNL* was no longer as wonderful as it used to be. Then in 1980, Michaels left the program and was replaced by network executive Dick Ebersol, who presided for five troubled years.

But in 1985, Michaels surprised a lot of people when the curtain rose on Act II of his reign as czar of *Saturday Night Live*. Brandon Tartikoff, then president of NBC Entertainment, had persuaded Michaels to come back. Tartikoff felt sure that only Michaels could recapture the irreverent, in-your-face magic that had made *Saturday Night Live* a beloved institution a decade earlier.

The big buildup to the return of the great genius was a little absurd, with echoes of Dolly Levi's return to café society in the big number with the waiters on the staircase in *Hello, Dolly!* And the advance hype was, of course, the perfect setup for a major letdown. In short, Lorne Michaels stepped up to the plate—and did not hit one out of the park for the home team.

All through the first season of Lorne II, his comeback was considered the disaster of the decade. And the media couldn't get enough of it. Had he lost his touch? Had he become too old, too flabby, too establishment, too irrelevant? The TV universe had changed a great deal between 1975 and 1985, and the shock value of irreverent satire had vanished. Other programs, other networks and other channels were delivering the outrageous, hip material that once had seemed to belong exclusively to *SNL.*

The 1985–86 season was such a bomb that for a while everyone assumed NBC would cancel the show after 11 years. But Michaels was above all a political survivor. So while a lot of people were sent on their way, Michaels held on. He had to be brutal—replacing virtually the entire cast—but his strategy worked. By the late 1980s, Michaels had recruited enough of the right new comedy stars—Dana Carvey, Kevin Nealon, Jan Hooks and Phil Hartman—to secure his dynasty indefinitely. Presto! The show rebounded and entered its strongest period since its first jubilant seasons.

In the case of Mike Myers, Michaels relied on a farm team that had helped him achieve success before—Canada's hidden comedy world. Michaels had grown up in Toronto and worked at the CBC before moving to New York; his ex-wife, comedy writer Rosie Shuster, was the daughter of Frank Shuster, who, along with his partner, Johnny Wayne, had raised the profile of Canadian comedy with his frequent appearances on the *Ed Sullivan Show*.

Two of the most popular performers in the very first season of *Saturday Night Live*—Gilda Radner and Dan Aykroyd—had come from Toronto's Second City ensemble at the Old Firehall. And there had since been a steady stream of Canadian talent following the trail from Toronto to Rockefeller Center in New York—including Robin Duke, Tony Rosato and Martin Short. In addition to the performers, there were many Canadians on the writing staff. Yet the Canadian influence was oddly subdued, almost subliminal. Canada was rarely mentioned on the show. It was almost as if the Canadian factor were a secret to be kept from the audience of *Saturday Night Live*.

Myers, who moved with Robin into an Upper West Side apartment on 84th Street, went through a stressful period of adjustment as part of the *SNL* machine. He had to get used to the odd requirement of doing creative work within what seemed like a committee of unwieldy size. And he had to succumb to the show's relentless schedule, which meant going from rough idea to final performance within a few days.

The ritual had been more or less the same since 1975. On Tuesdays, the staff of 15 or more writers drafted 30 or 40 sketches, and the cast contributed a few more. On Tuesday nights, the writers would typically stay up all night, like high school students cramming for finals.

Then on Wednesday nights, the cast and the writers squeezed into the writers' room on the 17th floor of NBC's headquarters in midtown Manhattan. They would be joined for the read-through by Michaels, other producers and crew members, and a few network officials.

Through some strange process that nobody really seemed to understand, a dozen or so sketches were chosen, and the rest discarded. Some veterans of the show thought the wrong choices were being made— that the best stuff was being killed while tame, mediocre fare went to air. The rap against Lorne Michaels was that more often than not he went for "safe and likable" over "brilliant." His advocates thought he was savvy enough to stay away from material that wouldn't be understood by many of the teenagers in middle America who made up the program's core audience.

On Thursday afternoons, the writers would return and gather around a long conference table, where they would dissect, word by word, each of the chosen sketches. And then they would get into the tortuous process of rewriting them—doing whatever they had to, to keep themselves going as Thursday nights inevitably turned into Friday mornings.

Fridays were always given over to rehearsal and final rewrites.

And before you knew it, the week was gone, there was a studio audience of 300 people ready to be entertained, and the guest host was yelling: "Live from New York, it's Saturday Night!"

No wonder the late Gilda Radner used to call this "an underrehearsed Broadway opening once a week."

Mike found that his Second City training served him well, but there was a big difference between his old stage job and his new TV job.

At Second City, it had seemed to him as if everyone worked at the same store. Now at *Saturday Night Live*, it seemed more as if all his colleagues worked in a small mall—but each at a different store. At Second City, the physical challenge was to keep going and get through eight shows a week; six nights a week; whereas at *SNL*, the pressure built all week toward a show that was performed only once.

"Working on *Saturday Night Live* is a combination

of *Das Boot* and *The Fantastic Voyage*," he once explained. "At Second City you're working on a smaller submarine."

According to the late Phil Hartman, it would have been easy to hate Mike—because he was phenomenally talented and blindingly prolific. But, Hartman added, he also happened to be the most likable and most modest person you could meet.

"Mike seemed so shy and self-effacing at first," Hartman explained to the *Washington Post*. "He was almost meek. But then came his first read-through and he was brilliant. Everyone vies for air time. We all want to see our material done."

For the first three weeks after he joined the show, Mike would do his writing at the office—sitting cross-legged next to the elevator bank—and wind up staying all night. He was terrified he was going to be fired.

Everything changed when, in his fourth week, Mike introduced "your excellent host Wayne Campbell" and his community cable-access show, originating in the basement rec room of the Campbell family home and co-hosted by Wayne's friend Garth, a techie and metal-head. Garth was played by Dana Carvey.

"I was completely surprised by the reaction," Mike observed later.

Almost immediately, Wayne and Garth became America's favorite comedy craze.

One of the first to offer celebrity validation was Henry Winkler, aka the Fonz on the old TV series *Happy Days*. Winkler called Myers and said that he loved the sketch, and that he hadn't seen a performer with such joy and abandon as Myers for an awfully long time.

Millions of people agreed. It quickly became apparent that Wayne Campbell was just what *Saturday Night Live* needed. Myers wrote these sketches with two members of the *SNL* writing staff, Bonnie and Terry Turner. The Turners were old friends and colleagues of cast member Jan Hooks, who had introduced them to Lorne Michaels. They struck up a rapport with Myers and became his frequent writing partners.

Wayne and his buddy Garth Algar are a pair of heavy-metal party animals—conceived by Myers when he was about 12 and spending a lot of time hanging around suburban rec rooms. The characters are composites based on five or six people Mike knew at the time.

"I used to be like Wayne," Mike would readily confess. Indeed, as a teenager, he had shared Wayne's fixation with those gods of heavy metal, Led Zeppelin and Aerosmith. And while he was in high school, he had added the babe-appreciating, fun-loving side of Wayne to the character.

But according to Alice Myers, her youngest son was not at any time remotely like Wayne. Indeed, Alice made no secret of the fact that of all the characters her famous son had created, Wayne was her least favorite. "He's sort of dumb," she remarked.

With slight variations, Myers had been doing his Wayne Campbell act for many years. For a while, he used to do it mostly to impress girls at parties and make them laugh. Later, he introduced Wayne to viewers of a Toronto TV show called *City Limits*. It was on a local station, Citytv, which probably came as close to the sensibility of cable-access television as any licensed TV station in the world.

Around 1987, Wayne Campbell became familiar to Second City audiences at Toronto's Old Firehall and to viewers of the short-lived CBC variety series *It's Only Rock 'n' Roll*.

But on *Saturday Night Live* there was one telling difference. Instead of broadcasting his Friday-night cable-access show from the basement of his parents' home in Scarborough, Ontario, on the fringes of Toronto, Wayne Campbell was now supposedly coming to NBC viewers direct from Aurora, Illinois, a suburb of Chicago.

There were people on the staff of *Saturday Night Live* and NBC who felt uneasy about admitting that Wayne and Garth were actually Canadian teenagers. The audience, they felt sure, would be much more understanding and accepting if these two dudes were more normal, that is, Americans. And so Mike was faced with the delicate problem of coming up with an American equivalent to Scarborough.

It happened that the only U.S. city Mike was familiar with was Chicago, where he had lived for almost a year. Chicago had many things in common with Toronto. It was a flat city on the Great Lakes; it was a city that was not New York but aspired to be; it was a city that had a comedy club called Second City; and it was a city that took hockey seriously.

In truth Mike and Robin had lived downtown in Chicago and had not made a habit of prowling the suburbs, but Mike imagined that some of them must be a lot like Scarborough, Ontario.

He asked Christine Vander, a writer from Chicago working on *Saturday Night Live*, for a Chicago equivalent of Scarborough. It had to be flat, and it had to have strip malls, factory carpet outlets, doughnut shops, gas stations and hydro fields. Without hesitation, she replied: "Aurora."

Even though Mike had never been to Aurora, the name rang a bell. He remembered from his Chicago days that Aurora was always mentioned in the carpet commercials on local TV channels. And, being the son of a man who sold the *Encyclopaedia Britannica*, Mike understood the mythical allusions to the goddess of light. Aurora, Myers imagined, was a tacky, sprawling suburb with a name that suggested delusions of grandeur. Perfect.

The participation of Dana Carvey created an interesting case of dueling egos. Garth, who seemed close to retarded, was essentially a sidekick character, but Carvey was the established member of the cast and he was much better known to the *SNL* audience. Obviously, Carvey contributed a great deal to the success of the sketches; yet he must have realized he was also getting into a situation where he would be perpetually subservient to a guy who was basically an unknown from Canada. Mike, after all, was not just Carvey's fellow performer; he was the creative whiz kid who had invented Wayne and Garth and the whole concept. This was a situation that almost guaranteed a clash of temperaments.

Within months, Wayne and Garth had become a popular and regular feature of the program. They struck a nerve with the audience in the great *SNL* tradition of John Belushi's "cheesebuggah," the Coneheads, Billy Crystal's "Mahvellous," Martin Short's Ed Grimley and Dana Carvey's Church Lady.

Delighted viewers savored catchphrases that Wayne was known for: "Excellent!" "No way! . . . Way!" "Not!" "She's a babe," "We're not worthy," "Right!" and, of course, "Party on!"

Because he was both a writer and a performer,

Mike had an even more demanding schedule than other members of the *SNL* team. He would often start writing a sketch at 3 A.M., working at his home computer until 8 A.M., and go to bed after faxing his material to the office.

By then, Mike was no longer doing all-nighters at the office. He had opted to do more of his work at home.

"Sleeping on a couch doesn't pay," he explained. "I'd rather sleep in my own bed."

8

BECOMING WORTHY

As NORTH AMERICA SUCCUMBED to the Wayne
Campbell craze, Mike Myers had to come to terms
with a certain irony. He had created the character as a
satire of youth culture, but now millions of people
latched on to it without quite getting the joke. They
took it not as a spoof but as a jocular homage to the
world of heavy metal; essentially, they agreed with
Wayne's take on the world. And of course it would
have been downright ungracious of Mike to suggest
that these followers were missing the point. What
performer who draws this kind of attention would

quibble over details of interpretation?

Wayne and his sidekick, Garth, quickly achieved cult status, and consequently they attracted some celebrated collaborators, adding to Mike's formidable profile. In one of the most famous episodes of the sketch, Wayne and Garth find a wonderful new reason to party on. Garth's cousin Barry, they discover, has worked as a roadie for the heavy-metal band most revered by Wayne and Garth—Aerosmith. And so one day, the boys in the band turn up at Wayne's house, just like that, for a guest appearance on Cable 10, Aurora.

It's all too much for Garth, who throws himself at the feet of the celebrity visitors while repeating, "I'm not worthy!"

In fact, Garth gets so wound up that Wayne has to remind him to take his Ritalin pills.

But even Wayne is a little overcome.

"Welcome to Wayne's World," he proclaims, bowing to the musicians and referring to them as "O mighty ones, greatest band in the world."

In one episode, Wayne and Garth compile a list of their top 10 babes. A few of the names are fairly predictable, including Julia Roberts, Farrah Fawcett and Kim Basinger. But a couple of the choices are startling and funny—Betty Rubble, of the Flintstones, and Josephine Baker, the famous black American jazz singer who conquered Paris long before most *SNL* viewers were born.

Almost unbelievably, one of the babes at the top of their all-time greatest list actually turned up to join Wayne and Garth one night.

We're talking, of course, about Madonna. In 1990 she gave Wayne Campbell a kind of celebrity endorsement by appearing in a fantasy sequence loosely based on her video *Justify My Love*. It's an indication of how worthy Wayne and Garth had become that Madonna didn't just agree to be on with them; she was the one who suggested it.

Mike was called on to kiss Madonna, and it was an uncomfortable experience, to put it mildly. Myers has always been a very private person. He tends to avoid public displays of physical affection. And he is not someone who goes around hugging people or likes being hugged by others.

This was the first time Myers had had to kiss someone in a dramatic setting. And it was hard to feel natural about it with all these people standing around watching them. So Mike said to Madonna: "I have to be honest with you. I don't know what to do. I'm, like, kind of new at this."

The way Mike recounted the story later, Madonna was really nice about it.

To demonstrate, she grabbed his hand and gave it a

tight-lipped kiss. Then she said: "Put your mouth on my mouth and pretend we're having a really good time." Jokingly, she added: "If you slip me the tongue, I'll kill you."

Madonna was so infatuated with Myers that she asked him to interrogate her for *Interview* magazine. After a few playful exchanges, she said: "Would you ask me some questions that have a resonance to my life? This interview is mostly about what you're interested in: toys and hockey."

Mike responded by asking whether she believed in psychics and wondering whether she had ever contacted the spirit world.

Mike's *SNL* episode with Madonna created such a stir that, for years afterward, he would be endlessly asked about it. In fact, he joked, it was usually mainstream Americans who wanted to know what it was like making out with Madonna. Kids at metal clubs were more likely to ask what it was like appearing on the show with Aerosmith. And what Canadian fans really wanted to know was not the answer to either of the above but how Myers had enjoyed playing hockey with that other Wayne—Gretzky, who once hosted *SNL*, providing a heaven-sent opportunity for the world's most hockey-crazed comedian.

Uncomfortable as his scene with Madonna might have been, it did no harm to the rising celebrity quotient of Mike Myers to be seen by millions of fans kissing the world's highest profile sex symbol.

Yet there were better reasons than that for Mike's increased popularity. His material was aglow with such energy and cheerful silliness, as well as genuine wit, that just recognizing him through his outlandish accent, makeup and costumes was enough to make people smile.

Most *Saturday Night Live* performers would have been thrilled if they could have achieved just one sketch character as memorable as Wayne Campbell, but Wayne was just one of what seemed like an endless stream of terrific comedy characters emerging from the Myers imagination.

In several cases, the odd characters Mike portrayed were an expression of his understanding and appreciation of British eccentricity, a taste he had acquired from his father, Eric, with his love for Monty Python, the Ealing comedies and Peter Sellers.

That side of Myers came through in a sketch called "Theater Stories," in which Mike created a deliciously pompous and affected host named Kenneth Rhys Evans, who presided over a TV panel of great lords and ladies of the British theater (with names like Dame Sarah Kensington), all desperate to top one another's backstage anecdotes.

In one episode of "Weekend Update," Myers got to

show off his uproarious impression of Mick Jagger, allegedly participating in a spirited debate on the PBS political program *Point/Counterpoint* with that other famous veteran of the Rolling Stones, Keith Richards. What agitates them is the headline news that a rock song about killing a cop has caused a furor, resulting in demands to have it banned.

Well, Mick wonders aloud, if you can't write a simple, innocent song about the joys of killing cops, what can you write about? And where will this distressing outburst of cultural tyranny end?

One of Mike's most brilliant inventions emerged from his experience in England working in children's television. "Simon in the Bath" was about an entertainingly warped little boy who seemed to take just a bit too much pleasure splashing about naked in the bath, with the excessively friendly smile of a hyperactive moron.

"I like to do drawerings," Simon explains in a precious voice that suggests years at an exclusive school.

As Myers explained when asked about the source of this material, he had always marveled at how well the English do childhood—with their Paddington Bears, chocolate toys and all that.

According to Myers, Simon was at least partly based on his English cousins who used to come to Canada to visit when they were growing up.

In one especially hilarious episode, Simon is joined in the bath by a new American friend—a kid named Vinnie, who, as played by Hollywood's favorite gremlin, Danny DeVito, talks like a baby mobster and has an adorable habit of pissing in the bathwater.

Where did Simon meet Vinnie? In Atlantic City, of course. And their topic was the wonderful Christmas Day they shared at the casino. From Vinnie, Simon learned a lesson that came as a revelation: "Sometimes Santa gotta get whacked."

Occasionally, Mike's obsession with British eccentricity revealed a dark side of him that few of his fans were aware of. That was the case with a bracing sketch about a wounded, soccer-loving soldier under care of a nurse/girlfriend, who, at first, seems devoted and loving. The poor bloke tries to keep his chin up in an uncomplainingly patriotic, Noel Coward sort of way, but his illusions are endangered when this trusted woman admits she has had his leg amputated.

Oh, and by the way, she has married another man, and given this spare leg to her new husband. This spouse enters, displaying a small mustache and looking disconcertingly like Adolf Hitler. It becomes evident that he makes surprisingly effective use of this extra limb he has been given, especially on the soccer field, which is bad news for the unfortunate British lad so determined to look on the bright side of every misfortune.

Sometimes Myers's characters had a bizarre scholarly or academic quality, which went along with their ebullient pop-cult energy—almost as if Mike had set out to invent loony-tunes for a postmodern comedy universe. One example was his prehistoric protagonist Lothar of the Hill People. Another was the ever-smiling and sadistic host of a lethal Japanese game show, in which a unilingual and increasingly hysterical American tourist, played by Chris Farley, is unwillingly trapped. Skits like this had a disturbing subtext that went far beyond what you'd expect to see on a mainstream network comedy show, and to which the only appropriate response was nervous laughter.

The sketches about Middle-Aged Man represented a kind of self-satire, because Myers was spoofing what he had become during his first season on *Saturday Night Live*.

In the course of eating all the wrong foods, Mike had gained 15 pounds, and his *SNL* colleagues constantly teased him. His response was usually to seem annoyed when anyone noticed his extra blubber.

Middle-Aged Man as played by Myers is someone who understands the importance of aluminum siding and the concept of escrow, and someone who has learned that when painting the garage, you must always start with a primer coat.

In one of the *SNL* sketches about Middle-Aged Man (formerly Young Man), Mike quotes one of his favorite authors, Kurt Vonnegut, on the subject of impotence. A middle-aged man, he explains, should feel grateful if he loses his sex drive because it's like getting off a wild horse.

Middle-Aged Man is a bit touchy and self-conscious. He's always asking accusingly, "You're looking at my gut, aren't you?"

He should not be confused with his father, Retired Man. One big difference: Middle-Aged Man knows how to hook up a VCR.

Apart from Wayne Campbell, the Myers character who drew the most attention from viewers was a dour, pouting German aesthete named Dieter—supposedly the German avant-garde host of a cultural television program called *Sprockets*, or, as Mike pronounced it in his fake-German accent, *Shprockets*.

Dressed in all black, with slicked-back hair and tortured posture, Dieter became famous for his severe taste in music and for crossing his legs in a peculiar, mannered way. From time to time, Dieter orders his crew to dance in a mechanical, robot-like way. What he likes to say is: "This is the part of the show vere we dahhnce."

But he is best known for the catchphrase: "Touch my monkey."

According to Myers, the character was based on a film student from Stuttgart, whom he knew in the 1980s.

"When I was young I hung out for a while in a sort of post-punk art scene in Toronto, the equivalent of Greenwich Village," he explained.

Myers says the real Dieter worked as a waiter in a pub in the Queen Street West area. He took Mike to a lot of galleries and movies. He was obsessed with textures, and said he always wanted to touch a monkey. Apparently, he also enjoyed touching tapioca and Styrofoam.

One thing Dieter and Mike had in common: They both loved hockey. Indeed, they used to trade hockey cards—until Dieter went back to Germany and then Australia.

"Dieter is the side of me that didn't go to film school," Mike once explained. "He loves obscure Americana."

In one of the most celebrated Dieter sketches Myers ever performed on *Saturday Night Live*, Dieter interviews octogenerian actor James Stewart—hilariously portrayed by Dana Carvey—and raves pretentiously about the actor's homespun rhymes.

"Your poems pull down my pants and taunt me," Dieter tells Stewart.

When asked why he had written a poem about his pet dog, Stewart tells a bizarre story about a prostitute in Mexico and a broken bottle.

Another sketch included clips from "Germany's most disturbing home videos."

From time to time, Mike would wonder what had ever happened to the real Dieter. He jokingly said that one day he expected Dieter to phone and say he'd just seen a sketch on *Saturday Night Live.* But that phone call never came.

During the summer, when *SNL* was off the air and on hiatus, Mike liked to spend as much time as possible in Toronto. And in August 1990, he made a rare appearance on stage at the Factory Theatre.

The reason was a cherished reunion with his old British performing partner, Neil Mullarkey. But while Myers had made sensational advances in his career since the two earned their reputation in London and at the Edinburgh Festival in the mid-1980s, Mullarkey was still mostly working on the same old, rather limited English comedy circuit.

In an advance interview with Craig MacInnis of the *Toronto Star* to promote the week-long run, Myers talked about how much he enjoyed being back in Toronto. He'd lived in London, Chicago and New York, but he confessed: "I'm really a bad homer." In Toronto, he explained, "you just seem to have a story for every square inch."

But why did Mike, having achieved stardom on *SNL*, want to do a grueling stage show at a small, distinctly unglamorous theater?

The answered seemed to be: to help Neil.

"The impetus of the whole thing is," Myers told MacInnis, "I think Neil's great. He's really funny, and he's a nice guy, and we work well together."

On stage at the Factory, where the twosome gave ten performances over eight days, Mike greeted the small crowd this way: "For some of you, this was a difficult decision. It was either this or the Ex."

Being a boy steeped in the folkways of a city sometimes called Hogtown, Myers was highly aware of that traditional end-of-August ritual, the Ex—aka the Canadian National Exhibition—which drew thousands of people to the Exhibition grounds near the waterfront.

According to MacInnis, who reviewed the show for the *Star*, "the program veered from farce to formalism and back, without missing a beat. . . . What the comedic pair offered was far more intriguing than the episodic whimsy Myers has brought to *SNL*."

Indulging their fondness for trashy Roger Corman films, Myers and Mullarkey developed a lurid plot line while they zoomed around a female volunteer, who was strapped to a chair. In the same vein, they did a spoof called "Attack of the Aliens," mocking the lovably tacky conventions of the genre.

The crowd was eager for a glimpse of the characters they knew from *Saturday Night Live*, and eventually

Myers succumbed to popular demand. Wayne Campbell made an appearance, telling the audience: "I'm a licensed babetician."

DOING A FUNKY LITTLE SHOW with Neil at the tiny Factory Theatre in downtown Toronto was a lark for Mike, maybe because he realized it was probably going to be his last shot at working beyond the fringe. He was already excited about plans that were afoot for his Hollywood debut.

Lorne Michaels was talking to Paramount Pictures about producing a movie version of *Wayne's World*, to be shot during *Saturday Night Live's* summer break the following year, in 1991. Mike was working on the script with Bonnie and Terry Turner, the husband-and-wife writing team who had collaborated with him on many *SNL* sketches. Joe Bodolai, a former mentor of Mike's from his days on the CBC variety series *It's Only Rock 'n' Roll*, also had a hand in the first draft.

Mike Myers would hardly be the first comedian to make the leap from *Saturday Night Live* to Hollywood. Back in the mid-1970s, shortly after the show had made its debut, several of its first generation of performers—including Eddie Murphy, Steve Martin and Chevy Chase—launched successful Hollywood careers.

But *Wayne's World*, the movie, was a nervy venture in many ways. In fact, Michaels and Myers would be attempting something that no one in the history of *Saturday Night Live* had ever pulled off.

Creating a character and doing a series of short sketches on TV was one thing; trying to sustain such a character for a feature-length movie would be much harder. Of all the famous *Saturday Night Live* sketches produced over two decades, only one had been turned into a full-length movie. And in the case of the *Blues Brothers* (1980), John Belushi and Dan Aykroyd had already appeared in several other movies.

Mike Myers was about to become the only comedian in history to make his Hollywood movie debut reprising a role he had made famous on *Saturday Night Live*.

9

HELLO, HOLLYWOOD

IN EARLY 1990, Lorne Michaels signed a production deal with Paramount Pictures, and he asked Mike Myers if he was interested in making a Wayne Campbell movie. The answer was an enthusiastic yes, and after a year of work on the script, the studio greenlighted the movie. The timing could not have been better. Brandon Tartikoff—the broadcasting guru who, as president of NBC Entertainment, had lured Michaels back to *Saturday Night Live*—was about to take over as head of production at Paramount. The deal was consummated, and Mike was on his way to Hollywood.

That journey would turn out to be the culmination of both his greatest dream and his worst nightmare. He would achieve stardom beyond his most expansive teenage fantasies; he would also face vilification, leaving millions of newspaper and magazine readers with the impression that Myers must be one of the most reprehensible forces ever known in the movie business.

But in the beginning, Mike's attitude was one of wide-eyed innocence.

"I'd always wanted to do Wayne as a movie," Myers recalled, "because that was how I always saw Wayne, as a character in a movie."

A Wayne sketch on TV was only 10 minutes, but despite the radical change in format, Myers did not find it hard to expand to a full-length feature film script. He felt comfortable writing a movie about Wayne, because he understood Wayne so well.

"I know the character because it was how I talked," he explained. "It was easy enough to explain what Wayne would do if he had a movie."

It helped that Wayne had a buddy; there was a rich tradition of lowbrow movie comedies about two likable morons, including the Laurel and Hardy series and the Abbott and Costello series. There was even a popular 1989 teen movie that had more than a few similarities to the saga of Wayne and Garth—*Bill and*

Ted's Excellent Adventure. And less successfully, there was *Strange Brew*, based on the McKenzie Brothers skits that Dave Thomas and Rick Moranis had created for *SCTV* in the early 1980s.

According to Myers, turning Wayne into a movie character was no big challenge. But he went about the task with his usual determination and obsessive concentration. Before starting the script, Mike studied a book on screenwriting. Then he blocked the story out on index cards. The hard part, he confessed, was keeping his material down to 90 minutes.

As far as Mike was concerned, Wayne's story was a chronicle of Myers's own experience growing up in Scarborough and Toronto—playing road hockey, taking the last bus of the night to the Tim Hortons doughnut shop, hanging out at the Gasworks (a favorite spot on Yonge Street). But beyond that, Mike took the opportunity to create an extended live-action cartoon. It would be both a parody of and a tribute to the popular culture of the 1970s and 1980s, crammed with inside jokes about the movies, TV shows and pop songs of those eras.

The movie had to be made for $12 million (U.S.)— a relatively small budget by Hollywood standards— with a tight shooting schedule of 36 days. Filmed in Los Angeles (doubling for Aurora, Illinois), the production had to be squeezed into seven weeks between late July and mid-September. There was no flexibility in the schedule; Myers, Carvey, Michaels and the Turners all had to be back in New York in time for the start of *Saturday Night Live*'s fall season.

To minimize the risk of turning over a movie to TV sketch comedy people from New York, Paramount hired Hollywood veteran Howard W. Koch Jr. as executive producer. Michaels and Koch jointly chose Penelope Spheeris as director. An awful lot had to be achieved in a short time, so it was crucially important to find a director who could move fast.

They knew that Spheeris—an outspoken redhead in her mid-40s known for edgy, non-studio movies—was tough. The daughter of a circus strongman who was murdered when she was seven years old, she'd supported herself working part-time as a waitress before graduating from UCLA Film School.

A key reason for choosing Spheeris was that she was one of the few film directors who could claim to be an expert on heavy-metal bands. She had just made the well-regarded 1989 documentary *The Decline of Western Civilization, Part 2: The Metal Years*. Aerosmith, the ultimate heroes of those headbangers Wayne and Garth, had actually appeared in her movie. And to Spheeris, Wayne and Garth were like fictional extensions of the real-life metal fans who had appeared in her documentaries.

"Very few other directors had heavy-metal experience," she boasted.

But there was another reason Michaels felt comfortable with her. He knew she could do comedy, because they had worked together on two Lily Tomlin TV specials in the mid-1970s, and Spheeris had produced short Albert Brooks films for the first season of *SNL* before going to Hollywood to produce Brooks's first movie, *Real Life*.

While she was being considered for the job of directing *Wayne's World*, Spheeris was also having discussions with the producers of another movie—a documentary about the criminally insane. But her priority was to have a chance to make her first studio movie. It would be a way of proving herself. She felt she needed to get out of the rut she was in, and she didn't want to go on being known strictly as someone who made dark, low-budget cult movies—such as *Suburbia* and *The Boys Next Door*, which were about rootless, troubled teenagers.

Though Spheeris might have thought going in that she would have a lot more fun on *Wayne's World*, things didn't necessarily turn out that way. Nor did her relationship with Mike Myers blossom into a mutual admiration society.

Here's how Spheeris put it after the shoot was over: "Dana was nervous because he had done pictures that had delivered less than he wished. Mike was nervous because he'd never done a picture. I was nervous because it was my first studio picture. Lorne was nervous because his previous movie, *Three Amigos*, didn't go to the top of the charts. And Paramount was nervous because they had all these nervous people involved."

Of course, there was no way of knowing in advance that the movie was destined to be a hit. And Mike, in particular, was terrified that it could be a humiliating flop.

Preparing to play Wayne on the big screen, Mike decided the time had come to shed his Middle-Aged Man extra poundage. So he checked into the Canyon Ranch spa and lost so much weight that his friends were alarmed.

Before shooting began, looking trim wasn't the only troubling matter on Mike's mind. Despite the fact that he was clearly the creative driving force behind the movie, he worried about losing control to one or all of the other people trying to assert their power. That included Paramount, Howard Koch, Penelope Spheeris, Lorne Michaels and Myers's supposed side-kick, Dana Carvey.

Mike had been thinking of limiting Carvey to a cameo appearance, but from Paramount's point of view, Dana was hotter than Mike at the time. He had been a standout cast member on *Saturday Night Live* since 1986, creating a sensation with his Church Lady routines and his dead-on impression of George Bush, Sr., who was then president. From Paramount's point of view, Dana wasn't just a sidekick, he was an essential element if the movie were to have a chance at the box office. But Carvey was also dangling another movie offer, and that put him in a strong negotiating position. Consequently, Carvey demanded, and got, a fee of $1 million plus a percentage of the net. That was almost double the $600,000 fee Myers was getting as an actor, although he had an additional fee as screenwriter.

Two weeks before the shoot began, Carvey threatened to back out, complaining that the script didn't give him enough to do. Paramount lured him back by promising him a chance to write additional material for himself. That did nothing to bolster Mike's self-confidence.

According to Lorne Michaels, on the first day of shooting *Wayne's World*, Myers was completely overwhelmed. The set did not look at all the way he had envisioned it, and the shock set off a panic attack. Michaels took him on a tour of the Paramount lot to calm him down. But despite constant attempts to reassure him, Myers remained in a state of nervousness, doubt, apprehension and agitation throughout most of the shoot.

The script was constantly being rewritten. There were something like 25 drafts, and that didn't count constant tweaking between drafts. Spheeris also had a hard time controlling her two lead actors.

"They're a different breed, comedians," she remarked. "There were times when I had to drag them in. They were having problems and didn't want to shoot."

Though learning the rules of the moviemaking game was a scary experience, Myers was delighted to escape from the creative limits imposed by the demands of live television. On *Saturday Night Live*, he was stuck in the studio. Ever since Mike was a child, he had fantasized about making movies.

Here's how he explained the making of *Wayne's World*: "They said, 'Do you want to do a movie?' And I said, 'Yes, please.' And I got to write and act in a movie."

But it wasn't quite so simple. Mike knew nothing about making movies, and that made him more anxious than ever. He couldn't believe he was getting away with doing this. He was haunted by the never-ending greatest fear of his life: that eventually, as he often joked, the no-talent police would come and arrest him.

That line was only partly a joke. Mike knew that regardless of talent, a lot of his phenonmenal success was a matter of luck. At Second City he had met many talented comedians who never managed to get a break, and never became rich or famous. Mike realized he was one of the truly fortunate ones, and he knew that his hot streak could come to an abrupt end. So it seemed important to enjoy it while he had it. On the other hand, the fear of losing that lucky streak was so terrifying and powerful that it almost paralyzed him— and sometimes gave the impression that being a big star was not a whole lot of fun.

The point of the movie was to tell the back story of Wayne and Garth. On TV, Wayne and Garth could never leave Wayne's basement. But for years, Mike had known in his mind what the rest of Wayne's world looked like.

He knew there would have to be a doughnut shop. And a heavy-metal bar. And that Wayne and Garth would drive around in a Mirthmobile (actually a pale blue Pacer with flames painted on the side and a can crusher mounted on the dash). And, of course, the plot would have to revolve around a babe or two.

The story goes like this: Wayne and Garth, a pair of long-haired teenage delinquents, emerge from a Midwest basement in search of metal music, parties and babes. Breaking out of cable-access TV, these two naive goofs move into the rarefied world of regional broadcasting—lured by a sleazy, snazzily dressed executive named Benjamin Oiler, who thinks they have commercial potential.

Benjamin is played by former Brat Pack actor Rob Lowe (who would later star as Sam in the prestigious TV series the *West Wing*). It was Michaels who thought of casting him, after Lowe appeared on *Saturday Night Live* as guest host.

The cast also features Brian Doyle Murray (as a corporate sponsor) and several of Hollywood's best-looking actresses, including Tia Carrere, Lara Flynn Boyle, Donna Dixon and Ione Skye. Carrere plays an aspiring rock singer named Cassandra, whom Wayne falls for after seeing her perform at a bar. Wayne is yearning for a new girlfriend after breaking up with a psycho played by Flynn Boyle.

Benjamin impresses Wayne and Garth with his swank 23rd–floor apartment, which they call a "fully functioning babe lair." According to Garth, chicks are powerless against Benjamin's power. And this over-the-top apartment is about as far as you get from Wayne's basement. Benjamin represents Wayne's nightmare—what Wayne could become if he sells out.

Wayne and Garth are overwhelmed when Benjamin gets them backstage passes and a private audience with their idol Alice Cooper at a big concert in Milwaukee. Standing in for the Midwest concert hall in the movie is the Universal Amphitheatre, where 400 extras create noise and action while Cooper growls out the lyrics of a song called "Feed My Frankenstein."

"I'm hungry for love," go the words, "and it's feeding time. Feed my libido."

Another R and R legend, Meat Loaf, did two days' work on the movie for a cameo appearance.

And the movie's soundtrack is crammed with metal classics from the 1970s, such as "Ballroom Blitz," "Foxy Lady" and Queen's "Bohemian Rhapsody."

Rob Lowe, who had gained a certain notoriety by making his own home porn movie, was an experienced film actor compared with Mike Myers. Lowe was the guy who helped Myers get accustomed to being on a movie set. As a result, the two bonded during the shoot, and, unlike many on-set alliances, theirs became an enduring friendship. It helped that the characters and milieu of Wayne's World reminded Lowe of his own boyhood in Dayton, Ohio.

According to Lowe, Myers was so green that "when they put a mark on the floor, Mike didn't realize he was supposed to stand there."

After all, there were no floor marks on *Saturday Night Live*. The TV show was shot with three cameras going simultaneously. Working on a movie—shot with one camera—was very different.

A lot of things were new to Mike, and Rob enjoyed tutoring him. For him it was fun to see the process of filmmaking through fresh eyes, and to enjoy watching Mike catch on to things and find his way.

After it was over, Mike would say: "I found out a movie is like a steamroller. You just have to keep moving, or it will crush you."

The production schedule was heavy, brutal and demanding. For Mike, one of the most difficult things to get used to was getting up as early as 5:30 A.M. All his life he had been a nighthawk. In high school, he was known for never attending any first-period class. Movie calls were early, and in Hollywood, Mike couldn't play hooky, even if he felt he was not at his best early in the day.

On the plus side, he enjoyed the space and the quiet of a film set as compared with *SNL*'s cramped TV studio in Rockefeller Center.

The worst torture for Mike was screening dailies as the footage shot the previous day came back from the lab and was available for viewing. He was beyond nervous. He would sweat right through his shirt.

"I'm always nervous," he explained. "Watching dailies almost destroyed me. It made me suicidal. Your big ugly mug is pasted up there, and it's hard to look at yourself. I hate the sound of my own voice."

There was a lot of emphasis on finding the right locations. What would Wayne's house and neighborhood look like?

One of the best scenes in the movie was also one of the most painful to shoot. That's the "Bohemian Rhapsody" sequence, with Wayne and the others in the car hilariously bobbing their heads up and down in time to the music. The scene resulted in a literal pain in the neck for both Myers and Carvey.

The script was constantly being rewritten, or as Myers preferred to phrase it, tweaked. At the suggestion of Lorne Michaels, it had been constructed in a modular way so that entire scenes could be dropped without causing any continuity problem.

Mike could get utterly solemn and obsessive about such details as the authenticity of his doughnut shop. During his Scarborough boyhood, the place where he hung out was named after Toronto Maple Leafs hockey player Tim Horton. In the *Saturday Night Live* sketches, the doughnut shops were named after Stan Mikita, who had played center for the Chicago Blackhawks.

As far as Myers was concerned, this was such an important part of Wayne Campbell's milieu that the real Stan Mikita was actually hired to make a cameo apperance playing himself in the movie. When Stan arrived on the set, he and Mike bonded immediately. Mike thought Stan was a wonderful guy, and the feeling was mutual. Mikita even had someone in his office send Mike a limited edition Mikita puck, which

Mike placed on his mantle at home, right next to his Wayne Gretzky hockey stick.

But then one of those things happened: Despite Mike's determination to keep Stan Mikita in the release version of the movie, Mikita's cameo wound up on the cutting room floor. Mike felt deeply embarrassed, but he also realized that in Hollywood, even when you create your own material, it's almost impossible to control what happens to it.

During the last weeks of shooting the movie, Mike was increasingly upset for personal reasons. His father, who had been declining for several years, had taken a turn for the worse and did not have long to live. To Mike, it seemed a cruel irony that Eric Myers—the man who had given him his ethos of silliness, the whole reason he had become a comedian—was going to leave this world without enjoying or even being aware of his youngest son's huge success.

Mike's gloomy preoccupation with Eric did nothing to alleviate tension on the set. And Spheeris made no secret of the fact she felt her contribution wasn't sufficiently recognized and appreciated.

After a couple of months in the editing room, Spheeris was surprised to discover how well the pieces fitted together, remembering as vividly as she did the mood of acrimony, fear and total chaos that seemed to pervade the set day after day, with scenes still being rewritten even as she was in the midst of shooting them. When it was all over, everyone, including Myers, Carvey, Michaels and Koch, gave Spheeris a list of suggested changes, and, of course, she was blamed for whatever suggestions she chose to ignore.

Spheeris liked to say that the experience of directing *Wayne's World* was a bit like going through an excruciating childbirth but winding up with a beautiful baby.

But no matter how pleased she was with the results, Spheeris sensed that if the movie became successful enough to generate a sequel, she would not be Mike's choice to direct again. Although Myers had tried to be courtly in his remarks about Spheeris in interviews, she suspected that his true opinion of her was: "She's not worthy."

10

THE SHADOW OF DEATH

By THE TIME ERIC MYERS DIED at the age of 69 on November 22, 1991, Mike felt as if he had already done his mourning for his father. It was more than four years since Eric had been diagnosed with Alzheimer's disease, and during that excruciating period, it had seemed to Mike as if he was losing his father one brain cell at a time. The smart, witty Eric who had lit up Mike's childhood slipped away long before the funeral.

The last year of Eric's life was especially painful, spent mainly in a hospital burn unit after Eric had run a scalding hot bath for himself—and then stepped into it. From Mike's point of view, Eric's personality had left his body at least a year before his official death. That meant Eric would never get to enjoy watching his youngest son become one of the world's favorite comedians, and he wouldn't be able to attend Mike's wedding.

Eric's death was a traumatic event, casting a large shadow over Mike's career. Ever since Mike was a little boy, he had idolized his father and aspired to live up to Eric's idea of great comedy. Much of what Mike had achieved was done for the sake of one goal: winning Eric's approval. Sometimes, it seemed to Mike as if the pleasure were less in the experience he was having than in anticipating the response he would get telling Eric about it afterward. Now with Eric gone, Mike had to wonder whether there was really any point driving himself to go on. Or, as Mike liked to put it in his own self-mocking way, he was bogged down in his "What's it all about, Alfie?" period.

Still, for a while Mike kept up his exhausting pace. He and Robin were back in Manhattan for the long, grueling *Saturday Night Live* season, though he was hardly feeling at his manic best. He was brooding about Eric much of the time, and having weird dreams—all the while planning a trip to England to comply with Eric's last wishes.

In the spring, along with his mother and two older brothers, Mike made the trip to Liverpool. The day after they arrived, they took a small boat from the Liverpool docks. Eric had been proud of the fact that he'd come from the town that gave the world the Beatles, and so, while scattering the ashes, Mike's brother Paul sang "In My Life."

Years later, Mike would remember the sound of the ashes landing on the water, and the seagulls surrounding their boat, and the rain that began falling afterward.

And he would say simply, "It's the best thing I ever did."

A few weeks after Eric died, Paramount held a test preview for *Wayne's World*. The audience was so responsive and enthusiastic that a number of key people connected with the movie and the studio began to realize they just might have a phenomenal hit on their hands.

That optimism was more than confirmed when *Wayne's World* opened on screens across North America on February 12, 1992—and instantly became a huge hit headed for a domestic box-office take well over $100 million.

Inevitably, after such a major success, life would change for Mike Myers, though he preferred to act as if nothing were going to be different. Just a few weeks before the movie opened, he flew back to Toronto to do some promotion. Within hours, he was hanging out with his boyhood friend David Mackenzie. Late at night, Myers, Mackenzie and a visiting Paramount executive donned skates and were shooting hockey pucks around a rink in North Toronto.

Predictably, some reviews of the movie were dismissive. Jay Scott in the *Globe and Mail* gave the picture zero stars, and in *New York* magazine, David Denby complained: "Everything gets repeated about 30 times, and no one changes or develops. What can you do with skit characters in a feature film?"

But the target audience hardly cared what the critics thought, and the picture gained a certain unplanned topicality through the death of Freddie Mercury, lead singer of the metal band Queen, shortly before its release. An even more important factor was that *Wayne's World* helped lift the gloom of winter at malls all over the continent. Not without reason. The material worked better as a movie than as a short TV sketch. Despite its repetitiveness, half-hearted story-line and scattershot jokes, *Wayne's World* turned out to be surprisingly funny and likable—a cheerfully cartoonish celebration of a pair of least-likely-to-succeed dudes doing their best to survive an upbringing of suburban blight.

The movie is part tribute and part parody, with bursts of energy and wit to keep it from being just another dumb teen genre flick. The script is a hyper-active, almost Joycean concoction full of wordplay, asides and knowing allusions to such pop culture icons as *Terminator 2*, Jimi Hendrix, *Twin Peaks*, *Star Trek* and *Scooby Doo*. There are so many jokes that the bad ones don't leave a stench; they just speed by harmlessly.

Part of what saves the movie is its cheerfully anar-chic attitude to movie conventions. Without being angry or bitter, it has a wised-up attitude to the corruption of product placement and formula enter-tainment.

And there's something winningly nervy about the way Wayne and Garth talk directly to the audience, in the manner of Richard III, and assume that the audi-ence is fully aware of how it gets manipulated by entertainers. When a shamelessly romantic interlude is tossed in, it's clearly labeled "gratuitous sex scene." And in case moviegoers don't care for the ending, the film offers a choice of three endings, along with a running commentary on each from Wayne, speaking straight to camera.

You could call those techniques Brechtian or post-modern if you wanted to put a fancy and academic spin on *Wayne's World*, but that would be false to its emphasis on fun. You could even see the movie as an ironic parable about youth alienation in the American hinterland, but that is not why people lined up for tickets.

Of course not everyone was disarmed, and there were a few niggling problems. As the outraged residents of Aurora, Illinois, pointed out, their town does not have California palm trees.

Mike was a bit taken aback when his mother phoned to say: "That Dana Carvey sure is funny."

He was even more taken aback when he learned how upset an ex-girlfriend was when she realized, while watching the movie with her new boyfriend, that her own painful breakup with the young comedian had become fodder for the script.

On screen a character named Tracy, played by Lara Flynn Boyle (who was later best known for playing assistant district attorney Helen Gamble on the TV series the *Practice*), encounters Wayne after breaking up with him, and gives him a present. The gift is a gun rack.

In the audience at a theater in Kingston, Ontario, Julia McKinnell was not amused. She was having an extreme case of déjà vu, because what happens in the movie is exactly what happened after she had broken up with Mike a few years earlier.

"How could he do this to me?" she asked in a newspaper article for Southam Press. "I was mortified."

The way McKinnell told the story, Mike was so self-absorbed when she knew him that they spent most of their time together discussing his performances. After a while, she grew tired of this routine and told Mike their relationship was over. He agreed they should part.

Weeks later, she had second thoughts. She bought him a present—a gun rack—thinking he would find it hilarious. He did not. He thought it proved she was demented.

Watching *Wayne's World*, McKinnell became especially upset when Wayne refers to Stacy as "a psycho hose-beast."

Since McKinnell's best friend happened to be dating Mike's brother, it wasn't long before the star and screenwriter of the movie heard about the incident. Which is why Julia McKinnell got an apologetic phone call from Mike Myers. He didn't realize she would be so upset. He should have warned her, he admitted. But he also kept saying the scene in the movie was funny.

She still wasn't laughing.

But millions of other people were. *Wayne's World* was not only outdrawing bigger budget movies starring Sylvester Stallone and Melanie Griffith, it had become a merchandising phenomenon. Even a video collection of Mike's sketches on *Saturday Night Live* became a hot item.

People in the industry who had been dismissive of what they regarded as a feeble, minor movie began to pay serious attention when they heard about the grosses. A deal for a sequel to *Wayne's World* quickly became inevitable, kicking off a round of heavy nego- tiating. The people who had worked on the first movie for modest sums were demanding huge fees. For those involved in the Wayne Campbell industry, the age of innocence was definitely over.

Mike, who always found something to worry about no matter how much success he was having, was apprehensive about being too closely associated with Wayne. He was eager to prove that *Wayne's World* was not the beginning and end of his comic imagination. And, indeed, he introduced an impressive range of characters in the course of doing *Saturday Night Live* for six seasons, with its weekly scramble for fresh material. There was one character above all that he was especially fond of, and that was Linda Richman, the host of a made-up daytime cable talk show called "Coffee Talk."

Linda is a New York Jewish matron with thick black hair, jangling jewelry, a major manicure job and a voice that positively vibrates with emotion when she talks about something she cares deeply about.

In fact, the character was based on Mike's mother-in-law, Linda Ruzan, a middle-aged divorcée from Queens who ran a commercial casting and research company called Hidden Talents. Mike found it gleefully funny how Linda pronounced coffee as "cawfee" and daughter as "dawtuh." That daughter, of course, was Mike's wife, Robin Ruzan.

One day, Mike put on his leather jacket. Linda cast an admiring glance at her son-in-law's attire and remarked: "It's like buttuh." Which prompted Mike to ask: "It's like WHAT?"

Linda Richman's favorite word is *verklempt*. That's Yiddish for "overcome by emotion." And the key to Linda's character is that's she's often *verklempt* by things like a new Barbra Streisand movie. And when Linda feels herself getting *verklempt*, she has a way of covering her mouth with one hand and using her other hand to send a signal that it's time to put the brakes on.

One of Linda's trademark phrases: "Talk amongst yourselves." It has to be uttered while gesticulating with an arm alarmingly loaded with bracelets.

Linda Richman made her debut on *Saturday Night Live* in 1991. By then Mike had been doing private imitations of his mother-in-law for the amusement of family and friends for three years—ever since they were introduced and she said to Mike: "Look at that *goyisha punim!*" (That translates as "Look at that Gentile face!")

In real life, Linda and Mike adored and amused one another. And in 1990, when playwright Jordan Ruzan,

Linda's son and Robin's brother, died in a car crash, it was Mike who pushed Linda into going on with her life.

Mike's lampoon of Linda was infused with love, but he wasn't sure she would be receptive to the idea of having Mike send her up on national television. In fact, she more or less dared him to do it. According to Linda, amusing as this running gag might be to their friends and family, the public would be completely indifferent.

Mike called her bluff, and, to put it mildly, Linda Ruzan was wrong. Linda Richman became an immensely popular figure who was often brought back for more episodes. By far the most famous episode was aired on February 22, 1992, when Mike, dressed in drag as Linda, was talking to Madonna and Roseanne Barr on "Coffee Talk." Their topic du jour: Barbra Streisand's new movie, *The Prince of Tides*.

Just as Linda, Madonna and Roseanne were discussing the movie, as well as Streisand's nails, Streisand herself appeared on the set, dressed in black pants, jacket and hat. No one was more surprised than Mike Myers. Barbra Streisand's appearance was a complete surprise to everyone except Lorne Michaels.

Shortly before the show went on the air live, Streisand had called Michaels to congratulate him on the success of *Wayne's World*, which was then in theaters. She happened to be in New York for the Grammy Awards.

Michaels invited her to do a surprise walk-on.

Mike was speechless. He might even have been as close as a WASP from Scarborourgh, Ontario, ever gets to being *verklempt*.

Whether Mike knew it at the time or not, his relationship with Streisand was destined to continue.

11

The Axe Falls

BEFORE HE WAS READY to undertake a Hollywood sequel to *Wayne's World*, Mike Myers had another movie to get through, a quirky, offbeat $20-million black comedy called *So I Married an Axe Murderer*.

The script, written in 1988 by Robbie Fox, had been making the rounds in Hollywood for four years. Set in San Francisco, it's the story of an unmarried poet who runs a bookstore. Fearing commitment and marriage, he has a disastrous romantic history. Then, finally, he meets and marries an attractive woman who owns a butcher shop called Meats of the World. She seems perfect—until he discovers evidence that she may be a serial killer.

The central character was originally Jewish, and for a while Woody Allen was thinking of playing him. Chevy Chase, Albert Brooks and Martin Short also gave it serious consideration. The flavor is suggested by one of this neurotic guy's big speeches in the script Fox wrote: "Some guys' wives are unattractive. Some guys' wives are unfaithful. My wife has a thing about murdering husbands. You have to take the good with the bad."

Fox's title was *Love and Fear*. Columbia Pictures had the script under option, and Fox kept writing new drafts as various stars and directors came in and out of the project. At one point Gary Shandling (of HBO's award-winning *Larry Sanders Show*) was set to star in it.

Meanwhile, Columbia executives kept debating whether the bride should be a killer or not. Finally, after Frank Price replaced Dawn Steel as chairman, Columbia dropped the project, and its sister company, TriStar, picked it up. Various other writers were hired to do new versions of the script.

After *Wayne's World* became a huge hit in February 1992, Mike was in a position to call his own shots, and he spent months sifting through the scripts he was offered.

There was only one he really liked and considered right for his sensibilities. He thought the premise was hilarious, and he was eager to play a more realistic character than Wayne Campbell. There was another, more personal reason Mike was drawn to the material. Fear of marriage was the subject of the script. And he was acutely aware that he and Robin, after living together for five years, both felt apprehensive about tying the knot. Marriage, the way they looked at it, was one of life's rites of passage. Unfortunately, it was the one that brought you closest to the ultimate rite of passage—death.

Mike realized that if he was going to make *Axe Murderer* without giving up his TV job, he would have to move quickly. In order for Mike to return to *Saturday Night Live* the following fall, the movie had to be shot during the summer. The deal with TriStar was announced the first week of June, thus ending four years of development hell and turnaround roulette for *So I Married an Axe Murderer*.

After months of speculation, *Variety* reported that Myers would star, Rob Friend and Cary Woods would produce, and the director would be Thomas Schlamme (who had directed only a few little-known movies, such as *Miss Firecracker,* but would later become prominent as a producer-director of the hit

TV series the *West Wing*). The role of Harriet, the possibly homicidal bride, was still uncast, as rumors that TriStar was about to sign Sharon Stone (famous for playing a murderous sexpot in *Basic Instinct*) turned out to be untrue.

The shoot would begin June 29 in San Francisco, so that Mike could finish working on the movie in time to return to New York for the start of *SNL*'s fall season in late September. That timetable left Mike feverishly rewriting the *Axe Murderer* script along with his old British comedy partner, Neil Mullarkey.

Before they tinkered with it, the script was a dark and complex look at fear of commitment and marriage. The premise—a guy falls in love with a possible murderer— was a cartoon metaphor exploring that subject. This is a guy who has always had bad luck with women; one of his exes was a kleptomaniac, and another, a member of the Mafia. Now, he is left to wonder whether he has just tied the knot with a crazed killer.

One of the main challenges for Mike and Neil as script doctors was to turn the poet-hero, Charlie Mackenzie, into a Mike Myers character rather than a Woody Allen character. They decided to change Charlie's background from Jewish to Scottish. That allowed Mike to draw from the "All Thing Scottish" segments of *Saturday Night Live*.

Myers and Mullarkey then reshaped the story into a broader comedy likely to appeal to the audience that adored *Wayne's World*. They didn't stop at doing minor touch-ups; they changed the tone of the entire script and many of the comedic moments within it.

Nancy Travis was cast as the innocent-looking but perhaps deadly Harriet, Amanda Plummer was signed to play her weird friend, and Brenda Fricker (the Irish actress who won an Oscar for *My Left Foot*) was set to play Charlie's mother. Anthony LaPaglia was signed to play Charlie's friend. But one piece of the casting puzzle remained. Who would play Charlie's over-the-top Scottish father, Stuart Mackenzie?

At least one well-known comedian was considered for the role, but then, in a couple of read-throughs, Myers took on the tricky task of playing both Charlie and his father. Everyone present thought Myers was hilarious doing double duty, and so the search for an actor to play the elder Mackenzie ended. In a way, this helped Mike to deal with the grief he was feeling over the death of Eric six months earlier, because he incorporated some of Eric's personality into the character of Stuart.

Mike liked the idea of playing a San Francisco poet, because he had a certain affinity with the so-called Beat writers like Jack Kerouac, one of Mike's favorite poets. And he was thrilled to have the chance to spend a summer in San Francisco. Indeed, in one on-set interview, he called San Francisco "the Florence of America" and explained that the whole city seemed like a wonderful set with a unified design in the shape of a pyramid, as if it had all been put together by the same art director.

Mike relished the chance to play a romantic leading-man role, even if it turned out to be a black comedy. Gone were Wayne Campbell's shoulder-length hair, torn blue jeans and grotty T-shirts. To prepare for the role of Charlie Mackenzie, Mike lost 20 pounds and got himself into shape. As Charlie, Mike had short-cut reddish brown hair and a dapper wardrobe. Before and during the shoot, he paid obsessive attention to his health and diet. He played hockey every day and, claiming he suffered from hypoglycemia, insisted on having a nutritionist on set to supervise his diet.

Playing two characters and also being in charge of the script proved to be a tricky and heavy burden, and there was a price to be paid. Once again there were rumors of clashes between the comedy star and his director, as there had been a year earlier on *Wayne's World*.

Mike was often holed up in his trailer fiddling with script changes for a scene that was about to be shot.

This created tension among various members of the cast and crew, and there was also a lot of talk about Myers's moodiness (he often seemed upset) and his obsessiveness about what food he should eat.

There was also a continuing debate between Mike and his director, Thomas Schlamme, who wanted to emphasize the realistic aspect of the script. Mike, who wanted to stress the comedy, at one point accused Schlamme of being anti-comedy.

After the shoot was over, Schlamme put it this way: "It's no secret this was a hard movie to make. Mike has a very strong point of view. That's his best trait and his worst trait."

Though Schlamme considered Myers a difficult personality, he felt that reports of trouble on the set had been blown out of proportion. Each man had a strong view of what the movie should be, each cared about the details and each argued vehemently. But it was unfair to say, as a number of people in Hollywood were saying, that *Wayne's World* turned Mike into a movie star and sent him spinning out of control. The fact is that Mike's attitude and way of working had been set long before he became a movie star.

In retrospect, Mike's view of the *Axe Murderer* shoot was that there had been 60 wonderful days and two bad ones. And what happened on those bad days?

"I was not a happy person, and I didn't get along with the director," Mike told Chris Heath of *Rolling Stone* magazine seven years later. "We had an old-fashioned disagreement that got personal, and it became the story of that movie."

Between the shooting of *So I Married an Axe Murderer* and its release, Mike returned to New York for his fourth season on *Saturday Night Live*. Probably the most memorable incident of the entire season was something that added to his controversial public reputation: a startling joke about the physical appearance of Chelsea Clinton, then a 12-year-old whose father had been elected president of the United States in November 1992.

In the aftermath of Clinton's victory at the polls, Chelsea suddenly became the object of tremendous media attention. And in a *Wayne's World* sketch, Wayne and Garth talked about Chelsea and suggested that she was less attractive than the daughters of Al Gore, the vice-president elect. As Wayne put it: "While it is true that adolescence thus far has been unkind, we think she's a future fox."

In general, the humor of Myers was characteristically silly rather than cruel, but there was a touch of meanness about this shot that had even Mike worried. A day or two after writing the sketch, he decided that line should be taken out. But some of the producers wanted to keep it in. The deal they made with Mike was that if the line got a laugh at the dress rehearsal, it should stay in. It got its laugh, and it stayed in.

By Monday morning, when everyone on talk radio was buzzing about Wayne's comment about Chelsea, Mike realized he had made a mistake. If there were any doubt that using the line on air had been a major error of judgment, that doubt vanished when Hillary Rodham Clinton, the First Lady to be, complained about the sketch.

Mike's point, he would explain in interviews later, was that Chelsea had acne, and Mike sympathized with her plight, because as an adolescent he'd been traumatized by his own acne. And he felt the sketch was meant to suggest that acne was nothing to worry about, and Chelsea would turn into a very attractive young woman. But that was not how a lot of people took it.

Mike was mortified to realize he had been misunderstood, and the sketch had been misinterpreted as a vicious attack. He was so upset about it that he wrote a letter of apology to Hillary Clinton.

Lorne Michaels did some damage control by explaining to the press: "We felt upon reflection that if it was in any way hurtful, it wasn't worth it. She's a kid, a kid who didn't choose to be in public life." Later the line was cut from the version of the show that was distributed for reruns.

Mike's letter of apology was not officially acknowledged, but word got back to him through unofficial channels that Hillary Clinton appreciated the apology.

Meanwhile, TriStar was nervous about *So I Married an Axe Murderer*, and the film's opening was delayed by several months (from March to July) while the studio tested it and tinkered with it. The delay merely intensified rumors that the picture was in trouble, though the studio tried to counter the negative buzz with upbeat explanations that, in fact, the movie was so strong TriStar thought it could compete with summer blockbusters.

In Hollywood, it is by no means unusual to hear writers complain that their brilliant screenplay was wrecked by meddlesome producers, and that their best stuff did not make it to the screen. And with a script like the one for *So I Married an Axe Murderer*, it would take Sherlock Holmes to figure out who contributed what, because the film lingered in development hell for years, during which time it passed through the hands of many potential directors and stars, all of whom wanted it rejigged to suit them. A number of writers were asked to mess with what the previous writers had done. So it should not have come as a shock to anyone that when the movie finally reached the screen, Robbie Fox did not feel his work was intact, even though he personally had written 15 drafts of the script.

More surprising was the venom and dismay with which a fairly routine tug-of-war about screen credits could become a huge moral issue subject to public debate every time Mike Myers agreed to do an interview. Somehow, the argument about who got what credit became all mixed with other industry gossip about the film. Previews were reported as problematic, and TriStar demanded changes.

Robbie Fox certainly acknowledged that the shooting script was very different from what he had originally written. His main character had been in his late 30s and bogged down in Jewish angst; Mike Myers wasn't at all like that. Fox was apparently displeased that the way things evolved, his material was turned into something, as he put it, on the level of *Wayne's World*.

It was no secret that Myers and his old pal Mullarkey had reworked the script to suit Myers's persona. That just happens to be the way the game is played when a star signs on to do a picture written before he arrived on the scene.

What really rankled Robbie Fox, evidently, was that Myers and Mullarkey didn't stop at rewriting. They had the nerve to suggest their work was extensive enough to merit an onscreen writing credit for *Axe Murderer,* which they proposed to share with Fox. Myers and Mullarkey made a formal claim through the Writers' Guild, and TriStar supported their position.

The decision of the Writers' Guild—based on a detailed analysis of different versions of the script—was that Fox deserved sole credit. But the fight wasn't over when the decision came down. Myers was upset about it and not willing to give up.

Fox received a phone call from Rob Fried, one of the producers of *Axe Murderer,* to let him know that Myers might be calling to negotiate a possible settlement. Then Marty Bauer, Myers's agent at the time, called to say it would put Fox in Myers's good graces if Fox agreed to share credit.

Finally, Myers himself called to ask if Fox didn't agree that the Guild decision was an injustice. Fox replied that, in his view, the judgment handed down by the Guild was the first thing that had happened on this project for a long time that was not an injustice.

Oddly enough, under the rules of the Writers' Guild, Fox would not have been at liberty to share credit at this point even if he had wanted to. But Myers felt so strongly he kept pushing. Some said it was because it was important to Myers to be taken seriously as a writer, not just as a performer.

Mike claimed he was more interested in getting a credit for his friend and collaborator, Neil, who had worked hard, deserved some recognition and would get a career boost from having his name on the screen.

The incident was a telling reflection of Mike's personality. When he felt strongly about something, he was tenacious, and he had a tendency to tune out the signals that, by continuing to fight, he was damaging himself. It was also part of the Hollywood syndrome that managers, agents and studio executives would rather do anything to keep a star happy than tell him something he might not want to hear.

Fox went public with his story, which quickly became a much-repeated bit of industry lore, and a central part of the continuing buzz about how difficult Mike was to work with, and about how honorable, hard-working writers are exploited by egomaniacal stars.

But when you watch the movie, it's hard to imagine that Myers and Mullarkey did not rewrite most of Fox's script. It may even be that, in the end, the biggest problem with the movie is that they didn't go far enough. The bits that seem most likely to have come from Fox are the ones that seem as if they should have been rewritten.

By the time the movie was finally released, in late July 1993, it was burdened with gossip about how much trouble there had been. Inevitably, much of the bad-mouthing surfaced in the pre-release publicity for the film.

Unfortunately, gossip about trouble behind the scenes was becoming the story of more than one movie. It was becoming the story of Mike Myers's career.

Michael Myers in *Range Rider and the Calgary Kid*
with David Ferry.
(COURTESY OF CBC)

Schwing!
Mike Myers and Dana Carvey in *Wayne's World*.

Hockey fan Mike Myers with Jason Priestly and Matthew
Perry at a L.A. Gear Hockey tournament.
(RON DAVIS/SHOOTING STAR)

Mike Myers at the Toronto Film Festival.
(TOM SANDLER)

In drag as Linda Richman on *Saturday Night Live*.

With Alice Myers (left) and Robin
and Linda Ruzan (right) 1996.
(RON DAVIS/SHOOTING STAR)

With Dana Andersen in Edmonton, October 2000.
(PERRY MAH/CP/*EDMONTON SUN*)

Embracing comedy mentor Allan Guttman
at Humber College benefit, April 1, 2001.
(COURTESY OF HUMBER COLLEGE)

Austin Powers in *Goldmember*.
(EVERETT COLLECTION/MAGMA)

Mini-me and Dr. Evil in Austin Powers.
(EVERETT COLLECTION/MAGMA)

Mike Myers gets a star on the Hollywood Walk of Fame,
July 2002.
(FRANK TRAPPER/CORBIS SYGMA/MAGMA)

Mike Myers as children's entertainer, Simon,
on *Saturday Night Live*.

Mike Myers poses with "Shrek", the character whose
voice he created, at the American International
Toy Fair in New York City.
(EVERETT COLLECTION/MAGMA)

Mike Myers in full makeup for *The Cat in the Hat* movie.
(EVERETT COLLECTION/MAGMA)

12

RUNNING ON EMPTY

In MID-1993, Mike Myers experienced two of the major passages of his life. In May, he celebrated his 30th birthday. That same month, he married Robin Ruzan after six years of living together. The private ceremony was in Toronto, Mike's hometown, and the couple kept it as low-key as possible—which was a lot harder to achieve than it would have been four years earlier, when he was a struggling actor.

To protect their privacy, Mike and Robin had to register at a Toronto hotel under assumed names. Then they flew to Paris for a honeymoon. Afterward, they headed for Los Angeles to prepare for the filming of *Wayne's World 2* and to do promotion for the release of *So I Married an Axe Murderer*. But selling this movie to Myers's fans would prove an impossible challenge.

The picture needed help, so Myers agreed to do a staggering number of newspaper interviews. And the journalists would ask questions like: "Why is Hollywood abuzz with reports that your ego is out of control?"

Myers had a standard answer to that one: "It's because I won the lottery. There are always two questions when anyone wins the lottery: 'Is he a nice guy?' and 'Is he gonna quit his job?'"

Reporters wanted to delve into reports of discord between Myers and his director. Thomas Schlamme claimed that reports of on-set warfare were exaggerated. According to Schlamme, Mike was under a lot of stress; he was playing two roles, and rewriting the script every day.

"I'm not trying to tell you that every morning we were hugging and dancing and having the best time of our lives," Schlamme told the *Los Angeles Times*. "This was a very hard movie to make. But the notion that after Mike did *Wayne's World* he turned into this demon has been blown out of proportion."

In an interview with Jamie Portman of Southam Press, Mike confided: "I read all the stuff about me—

and it really hurts." According to Myers, his troubles stemmed from the fact that *Wayne's World* grossed $121 million (U.S.)—and turned him into the kind of star who is an easy target. "The whole thing has been a bizarre ride," Mike remarked. "It's very, very freaky. Now I find myself in my car and see this familiar-looking face on the side of a bus shelter, so I pull over furtively and discover that, yes, that's really me on the poster."

Along with the bewilderment and disbelief Mike felt about this kind of fame came a dose of pain and sorrow. "When your film is a big hit," he explained, "what happens is that a lot of things get written about you that are negative spins."

Still, Myers had his allies in *Axe Murderer* producers Robert N. Fried and Cary Woods. "I'd work with Mike again in a second," said Fried.

"I've never been in a situation like this," Mike sighed. "There's a spin being put on everything I do or say." Example: Mike goes out to buy milk, but after he gets home, he finds it's sour, so he takes it back. Then comes the negative publicity spin: Mike Myers has a milk hang-up.

"It makes you just want to drink the sour milk so you don't have to deal with that," Mike concluded.

The reception to *So I Married an Axe Murderer* turned out to be bracingly sour as well.

Mike's fans were hoping for another *Wayne's World*. Instead, they got a somewhat charming, mostly messed-up and definitely offbeat romantic comedy about a mild-mannered poet with commitment issues.

The most enjoyable element in the movie was Mike's performance as Stuart Mackenzie, the hero's crackpot father. The role gives him a chance to banter with the hilariously bawdy Brenda Fricker.

"Give yer mother a kiss or I'll kick yer teeth in," the hyperactive and possibly deranged Stuart orders his son. He makes a point of paying serious attention to his Scottish heritage, which includes a bagpipe rendition of "Do You Think I'm Sexy?" After too many drinks, Stuart likes to sing along to Rod Stewart and the Bay City Rollers.

Unfortunately, Myers as Charlie Mackenzie, the neurotic bachelor who shouts his terrible poetry into a nightclub microphone so he can be heard over the jazz combo, is far less inspired. Charlie is just a bit too ordinary.

Myers has some likably low-key scenes with Nancy Travis, and she is charming as Harriet. But the script becomes tiresome once the audience realizes that (a) he suspects her of being a murderer; and (b) she's innocent. If there's a way to make this work, Thomas Schlamme doesn't find it; the most obvious fact about his work as director is that he entirely lacks the sense of pacing needed for this sort of oddball comedy.

Still, the box-office performance of *So I Married an Axe Murderer* was worse than anyone anticipated. Despite a very broad midsummer release, the picture took in only $12 million (U.S.)—roughly 10 percent of the take that *Wayne's World* enjoyed.

Mike, who was shooting *Wayne's World 2* when *So I Married an Axe Murderer* hit screens across North America, was devastated. The picture's box-office failure would haunt him for years to come, and make him more apprehensive and insecure than ever when embarking on risky new ventures.

Given the spectacular box-office success of *Wayne's World*, a sequel was almost inevitable. As Lorne Michaels explained, after the first record-breaking weekend of the film's release, "people who hadn't been paying much attention started to pay a lot more attention."

But *Wayne's World 2* turned out to be far from an easy ride. For one thing, there was a lot more pressure and a lot more at stake. No one had been expecting much from the first *Wayne's World*, and its budget reflected that; those involved had been willing to work for relatively small fees. But, *Wayne's World 2* was burdened with great expectations. And after the bonanza of the earlier film, everyone involved demanded to be well-paid.

Creatively, Mike faced some challenges. Wayne and Garth had been teenagers when Myers and Carvey began playing them in 1989, but by now they were obviously older. So just exactly how old were Wayne and Garth? How long could they go on being perpetual adolescents? Mike knew he had been lucky to get by with the first movie, extending a TV sketch into a feature film. So where was he going to find material for a second movie?

The answer, Mike decided, was in an old British comedy that his deceased father, Eric, had loved. It was a 1949 Ealing Brothers comedy called *Passport to Pimlico*, starring Stanley Holloway. Mike asked Paramount to get the rights to the movie, and he wrote a script—in which Wayne Campbell acquires his own country.

But only weeks before shooting was to begin, Mike got word from the legal department at Paramount that the movie couldn't be made. One Paramount regime was on its way out and another on its way in. And somehow, nobody got around to nailing down the rights to *Passport to Pimlico*.

For a while, it appeared there wasn't going to be any *Wayne's World 2*. But Sherry Lansing, who had just become the studio's head of production, was adamant that Myers had to live up to his obligation to come up with a movie. And after a certain amount of pressure and delay, he did. With the help of his old writing partners, Bonnie and Terry Turner, Mike quickly wrote a new script in which Wayne and Garth organize their own music festival—an event very much like Woodstock.

The picture was shot during the summer of 1993, while *Saturday Night Live* was on hiatus. Dana Carvey came back to play Garth, and the cast included Kim Basinger, Drew Barrymore, Christopher Walken, Charlton Heston, Heather Locklear and Chris Farley.

Penelope Spheeris, who had directed the earlier *Wayne's World* movie, was not invited to direct this one. Instead, Myers and Lorne Michaels drafted Toronto-based Stephen Surjik, who had worked extensively with Michaels on the *Kids in the Hall* TV series.

They had a good time making it, but the picture was not destined to re-create the box-office magic generated by the original.

The subject of arrested development, which had formed the subtext of the *Wayne's World* sketches right from the beginning, became the dominant theme in *Wayne's World 2*. Midway through the movie, a lot of people found themselves scratching their heads and asking: "Now wait a minute. How old are these guys anyway?"

In the beginning, Wayne clearly had been a metalhead teenager, and there was no problem of believability, because Mike was almost the same age. But by the time *Wayne's World 2* was filmed, Mike had passed his 30th birthday—and he looked his age.

At this stage, Wayne and Garth seemed too old to be drifting along aimlessly, and it was clear they were never going to grow up. Indeed, the material had once seemed refreshing because you could feel safe from the corny conventions of "coming of age" movies with their excruciating lessons in the art of living. *Wayne's World* liberated us from that muck; the audience could enjoy the frankness of the characters and their lack of any discernible interest in becoming wiser and more mature.

Yet at a certain point, as it became apparent that Wayne and Garth were really too old for this kind of cheerful irresponsibility, some people in the audience may have started to feel conflicted and uncomfortable. By laughing and enjoying the characters' escapades, were we perhaps giving our seal of approval to real-life loafers who cling desperately to their adolescent ways, even as they move into their fourth decade?

In *Wayne's World 2*, Wayne confesses that he feels as if he's in a John Hughes rites-of-passage movie. And he undertakes a kind of spiritual quest—a dark journey through the rock 'n' roll past—following instructions from the late rock legend Jim Morrison, who appears to him in a dream. It is at Morrison's suggestion that

Wayne and his pal Garth stage Waynestock.

This plotline has something to do with Mike's own yearnings and feelings about his growing-up years in Scarborough. He lamented the fact that he was born too late to get in on Woodstock (he was six in the summer of 1969), so the idea of Wayne's producing his own Woodstock festival seemed deeply satisfying, as well as funny. In a way, this was Mike's tribute to the turbulent decade he was born into, the 1960s. At the time, he had been too young to understand and enjoy the era. Similarily, this manifestation of Mike's obsessive need to sort through the rubble of 1960s pop culture and reinvent it for himself in a loving but satirical way makes *Wayne's World 2* seem, in retrospect, like a precursor of *Austin Powers, International Man of Mystery.*

Wayne and Garth keep coming across pop-cult artifacts, such as an old "Frampton Comes Alive" LP album, while trying to plan their show. Showing the album to his girlfriend, Cassandra (once more played by Tia Carrere), Wayne explains: "If you lived in the suburbs, you were issued it. It came in the mail with samples of Tide."

And there's a Gerry and the Pacemakers record, which gives Wayne a chance to quip: "You know, I bet those guys actually have pacemakers by now."

Wayne's World 2 is even lighter, more relaxed and

more enjoyably silly than its predecessor. It has a
disjointed, casually thrown-together quality that
seems as marvelously effortless as the series of *Road*
movies (such as *Road to Rio*) that Bob Hope and Bing
Crosby used to do in the 1940s and 1950s, or the two
comedies Richard Lester made with the Beatles in the
1960s. The jocular movie parodies and pop-culture
allusions fly by so quickly that disposability seems like
a heightened state of being. The giddiness reaches a
plateau when a whole chorus of street people break
into the theme song for the YMCA.

Even big-name stars seem to come and go in easy-
to-use mini packages. James Wong Howe as
Cassandra's father turns a martial arts contest with
Wayne into one of the film's most hilarious sequences,
thanks to the witty new way dubbing and subtitling
are used. Kim Basinger is funny and foxy as the bomb-
shell who tries to seduce the ever-sly and enigmatic
Garth. An appropriately sinister Christopher Walken
does a quick bad-guy turn as the shady record
producer who lures Cassandra away from Wayne with
promises of a Hollywood breakthrough. A rock band
with divine status, Aerosmith, provides genuine
history-of-rock-'n'-roll status. And in case you don't
like its first stab at an ending, the movie backtracks
and provides another option. *Wayne's World 2* is, above
all, a movie whose restless wanderings are completely

understood by anyone addicted to channel-hopping.

As for the Woodstock connection, well, it's perceived from the point of view of people who are too young to remember the era when it happened but have heard a lot about it from their parents. Wayne and Garth, we learn, saw the movie *Woodstock* in a high-school history class. And it kind of bothers Wayne that the young hippies on screen in Woodstock have by now taken over running America.

But certain points about Wayne and Garth remain forever vague. When, exactly, were they in high school? Did they graduate? At what age does it become a bit of an embarrassment if you have no interest in life beyond attracting babes, drinking beer, listening to heavy-metal bands and partying? If Wayne and Garth are still like this when they hit 40 or 50, will they seem like the kind of pathetic losers that no one finds entertaining?

These were questions that would presumably remain unanswered for some time, because the *Wayne's World* franchise pretty well used itself up with the release of this movie sequel. When *Wayne's World 2* was released in December 1993, it seemed at first as if it could be another box-office winner. The sequel took in $14.2 million (U.S.) in its first weekend at theaters across North America, which was close enough to the staggering $18.1 million the first

Wayne's World picture had grossed in its opening weekend almost two years earlier. But whereas the first *Wayne's World* movie had then gone on to an amazing take of more than $150 million, *Wayne's World 2* lacked what is known in the film business as "legs." Attendance dropped off steeply and the picture wound up earning less than $50 million (U.S.)—a lot less than Paramount was counting on.

In any case, Mike was getting embarrassingly old to play this role. And given the lackluster commercial performance of the movie, nobody was going to pressure him to go on doing it.

13

VERKLEMPT

IN EARLY 1994, shortly after the release of *Wayne's World 2*, Mike Myers experienced the greatest psychic meltdown of his life. The failure of the sequel to come anywhere near the numbers achieved by his first movie—coupled with the disastrous record of *So I Married an Axe Murderer* less than six months before—meant that Myers was no longer regarded as the hottest star in Hollywood.

For years, Mike had joked that one day the no-talent police were going to come and arrest him, and now his worst fear seemed to be coming true. He had been tried and convicted of the most horrific crime imaginable in the universe of Eric Myers: not being funny enough. It followed that Mike, who was not yet 31 years old, had to face the very scary possibility that having achieved sensational, almost undreamt-of success at a ludicrously young age, he might have peaked early and quickly segued into his declining years.

Emotionally, Mike had been living on an overdrawn account for a couple of years. Eric's decline and death in the fall of 1991 would have been devastating no matter what, but they were more so because Mike hadn't had time to absorb what happened. Two days after Eric died, Mike was back in New York appearing on *Saturday Night Live*. A day or two after Eric's funeral, Mike was on a plane to L.A. for the first test preview of *Wayne's World*. Alice Myers was adamant that the show must go on. And her youngest son did a persuasive job of going through the motions. His heart was broken, but his schedule didn't include time to grieve.

There was another family tragedy to deal with—the shocking death of Robin's brother, Jordan Ruzan, in a 1990 car crash.

As far as Mike was concerned, it was too much, too fast. He needed to get off the roller coaster. That his career was in downturn mode was actually a kind of opportunity. It gave him a chance to drop out. The tipoff that dropping out was precisely what he meant to do came in the spring of 1994, when Mike finally bailed out of *Saturday Night Live* after six seasons.

The decision wasn't based on getting a better offer to work elsewhere. It was based on Mike's feeling that enough was enough—and that work wasn't what he needed to focus on at the moment.

It was also based on Mike's realization that his stardom had carried too high a price, that he was missing out.

Bill Murray, another *Saturday Night Live* alumnus, had told Mike how much he'd enjoyed a two-year mid-career break, during which he studied French at the Sorbonne. Paris wasn't what Myers had in mind, but the idea of a break was appealing.

Mike wanted to spend more time with Robin. They went to Liverpool and visited his aunts, who lived in a series of contiguous row houses. They traveled around Europe for a while. And when they got back to L.A., they decided they were ready to nest.

Mike and Robin saw a lot of Rob Lowe and his wife, Sheryl Berkoff. When they visited the Lowes at their L.A. house, Mike suddenly realized that it was possible to be a performer and, at the same time, have something resembling a normal life, with such fringe benefits as a dog and a backyard.

Mike and Robin had been constantly on the move, and living out of suitcases had become a way of life. Discussing the lifestyle of the Lowes, Mike told Robin: "I want that."

And so they bought a house in the Hollywood Hills. Mike, who had been a voracious reader when he was younger, rediscovered the pleasure of having time to read books. He took power-skating lessons and played hockey three times a week at the Iceoplex Arena in the San Fernando Valley. There was time to go to the theater, and to practice chords on his new guitar.

Was Mike depressed? Well, even at the best of times, he was not, in his personal life, a happy-go-lucky clown. Comedians rarely are. Mike was painfully shy and reserved. He worried a lot. But now he was more subdued than usual, even morose.

Looking back a couple of years later, here's how Mike viewed this period: "I'd always reported in to my dad about everything I had done, and suddenly he was gone and it was really hard for me. Nothing seemed to matter. So much had happened all at once, and it hadn't really been so long before that I had just been this guy who lived in an apartment above a Korean grocery store in Toronto."

Though Wayne Campbell was a character Mike could no longer play, he did go on playing Linda Richman even after his departure from *Saturday Night*

Live. Following Barbra Streisand's surprise appearance on a "Coffee Talk" segment of *Saturday Night Live*, Streisand was eager to continue her association with Mike/Linda.

She found a way. On the last night of 1993 and the first night of 1994, Streisand returned to the concert stage for the first time in 22 years. The venue was the MGM Grand Hotel in Las Vegas. Both shows were sold out months in advance, and the two concerts set a box-office record: $12 million over two nights. Among the 26,000 who filled the hotel's arena were Michael Jackson, Steven Spielberg, Mel Gibson, Michael Crawford, Alec Baldwin, Kim Basinger, Quincy Jones and Peter Bogdanovich. Ticket prices ranged from $50 to $1,000, and scalpers were getting $5,000 for a top ticket.

Streisand sang "People," "Evergreen," "The Way We Were" and "He Touched Me." But nothing delighted the crowd more than a surprise appearance by the world's biggest Streisand fan—Linda Richman—who bantered with her idol, and of course did not forget to mention that Barbra had a voice "like buttah."

At a rehearsal before the show, Mike introduced Barbra to the real Linda—his mother-in-law. Not surprisingly, Linda Ruzan was *verklempt.*

"I waited 30 years to meet you," she told Streisand. "But I'm going to kiss my *daw-tuh* first."

Then, just to regain her equilibrium, she walked over to kiss and hug Robin and Mike. This served the same purpose as saying "Talk amongst yourselves." It gave her time to settle her nerves.

When Barbra reacted by kissing and hugging her, Linda was beyond *verklempt*. The thought that flashed through her mind was "Oh my God, this is more than I can bear."

Streisand followed her Las Vegas triumph with a concert tour, and Mike/Linda became a semi-regular part of the show, joining her on parts of the tour.

During this period, Robin, who had always colla-borated with her husband on "Coffee Talk" sketches for *Saturday Night Live*, started work with Mike on a screenplay about Linda Richman. The movie was going to be called *Linda Goes to Israel*. Mike and Robin were quite excited about the project, and there was even a bidding war. Warner Brothers beat out Disney and New Line Cinema by putting up $500,000 (U.S.) up front.

But as *Variety* reported in January 1995, the studio was upset about the budget. Warners wanted to cut it from $22 million (U.S.) to $18 million, and sent Myers back to revamp the script accordingly. After Myers had cut some characters and locations, some Warners executives felt the script had been watered down too much, and no longer wanted to make the picture.

Mike might have been able to get it going at another studio, but his feeling was that Linda Richman's moment had come and gone.

Then one day in 1995, Mike came up with a more exciting idea for a movie: a comedy about the collision of 1960s pop-cult mythology with the 1990s. It all started when, driving to hockey practice, he heard an old song by Burt Bacharach, "The Look of Love," on his car radio. Something clicked in Mike's head. His first reaction was: "God, I love this song, and I love everything it implies."

What it implied was the swinging 1960s and London, the ultimate switched-on city of the era, with such distractions as the fashions of Carnaby Street and decadent parties. The associations that came to Mike's mind included Matt Helm, Ursula Andress, *Casino Royale*, private jets with minibars and, of course, both James Bond and the actor most strongly associated with the role: Sean Connery.

Before long, Mike was talking in the lingo of the '60s, with mocking quotation marks around every phrase: "Hey, baby, how are you? Let's go shag."

Robin knew something was up when Mike got into the habit of walking around the house and saying weird things to her, such as "Do I make you horny?"

Finally, wanting to escape from taking part in a goofy game, she suggested that he write a script rather than waste his best lines on her. Mike spent the next four weeks writing it all down. That's how Austin Powers—swinging fashion photographer by day, daring spy by night—was born.

Austin Powers: International Man of Mystery was Mike's spoofy take on James Bond and other supercool sleuths of the swinging '60s. Only Austin had bad hair, bad teeth and bad pickup lines. And, of course, he practically invented the verb "to shag," which put satirical quotation marks around the steamy sexual liberation of the 1960s.

Where did the name Austin Powers come from? Well, it sounded a bit like Aston Martin, the kind of car James Bond liked. And Mike liked the idea of having the character say: "Powers by name, powers by reputation."

Emotionally, creating Austin Powers was a tremendous act of catharsis for Mike, because it was a huge posthumous tribute to the obsessions of his departed father.

Eric Myers adored James Bond movies, along with his other favorites of British pop culture, such as the Avengers, Peter Sellers, Alec Guinness and Monty Python.

A spoof of the swinging private eye allowed Mike to indulge in exactly the kind of silliness that Eric adored. It was a way for Mike to wink at all the old

British movies and TV shows that had flickered from
the TV set in the Myers living room while he was
growing up.

Austin Powers: International Man of Mystery was
conceived as the tale of a world-class playboy and
part-time special agent who, after 30 years in a
cryogenic state, is thawed to match wits with his
nemesis, Dr. Evil. The movie is a lampoon of swinging '60s absurdities: free love, psychedelic music,
clothes in rainbow colors. But this is not a satire or a
critique of the era. It's an attempt to use those artifacts
to reach a blissful state of silliness—a world of bizarre
childishness like the one director Tim Burton helped
that ultimate childlike performer, Pee-wee Herman,
create in the movie *Pee-wee's Big Adventure*.

Austin Powers may be a superspy, but he conspicuously lacks Sean Connery's sexual charisma. Mike's
version of the ultimate British spy is notable for his
thick glasses and cheesy bell-bottom pants. That's why
his raging libido seems so laughable.

While coming to terms with his badly dated ideas
about swinging, Powers has to go head to head with
Dr. Evil. The British intelligence authorities bring
Austin Powers out of the freezer to fight the demonic
enemy again. What he doesn't grasp is that the
cultural landscape has changed; he's still behaving as if
the '60s never ended.

Around the time that Mike was writing his first draft of the *Austin Powers* script, he and Robin would often have dinner with her friend Susanna Hoffs, a singer, and Susanna's husband, Jay Roach, an aspiring cinematographer and screenwriter who dreamt of directing a movie.

Mike and Jay had certain things in common. They both liked to talk about the philosopher Joseph Campbell and his notion that storytelling is a universal experience—that the need to tell stories is what connects one person to another. They were both addicted to the History Channel.

At one point, Mike invited Jay to take a look at his script for *Austin Powers*, and also asked for his ideas on who could direct it. Roach was a self-confessed workaholic from New Mexico, whose life had been changed when, as a pre-law student at Stanford, he saw Woody Allen's *Annie Hall* and decided he had to make movies.

Mike tried out some of his Austin Powers material by performing it at the Groundlings Comedy Theatre in L.A. and invited Roach to join the audience. According to Roach, Mike's first script was too specifically derived from the Bond films.

"We sat down and re-imagined it," Roach explained a few years later. "We watched a variety of films that were sort of '60s pop art to inspire us."

Among the films they watched: Woody Allen's *Sleeper*, Michelangelo Antonioni's *Blow-Up*, and a couple of lesser-known thrillers, *Danger: Diabolik* and the *Tenth Victim*.

"All these films had incredible style to them," Roach explained. "And I thought: 'Why can't style be funny?' So we re-imagined *Austin Powers* as a pop-art comedy."

According to Roach, the objective was not to spoof a genre but to embrace the best parts of it and put the stamp of Mike's unique personality on it. In Roach's view, he and Myers were like DJ Mixmaster guys trying to sample the most interesting parts of different things and combine them with their own flavors to create something new.

Mike De Luca, then production chief of New Line Cinema, heard a pitch for the movie and liked it enough to commit to produce it with a budget of $16 million.

"*Austin Powers* is one of those laugh-out-loud scripts," said De Luca in making the announcement. "This a unique film character, and we are looking at this project as a potential franchise for the company."

He got that right.

Roach was giving Myers suggestions about possible directors. After several months, Mike still hadn't found a director. He decided to approach New Line and ask if Roach could be hired.

New Line executives were less than thrilled by the suggestion. "Who is this guy?" they asked. Roach put together a reel of the projects he had worked on. Robert Shaye, co-chairman of New Line, told Roach: "Nothing in your reel suggests you're funny and can direct a comedy."

To win him over, Roach prepared a scene-by-scene breakdown of the movie, presented some outrageous costume designs, and performed parts of the material with Mike. At the end of the meeting, Shaye said: "Okay, you have the job."

Looking back on that meeting, Roach marveled: "It was an incredible act of blind faith on the part of Mike. He put his whole career on the line for me." New Line trusted Myers, and that turned out to be a smart decision.

The material gave Myers and Roach a chance to indulge themselves in campy excess as they depict Austin's garish world, with its puffy shirts and velvet trousers. Austin comes across as the kind of guy who has spent altogether too much time reading *Playboy* and trying to emulate Hugh Hefner. Adding flavor to the overripe atmosphere are Michael York as Austin's supervisor, Mimi Rogers as his partner, Mrs. Kensington, and Robert Wagner as Dr. Evil's right-hand man, complete with an eyepatch and a white tux.

Even more inspired than Myers's creation of the title character is his Dr. Evil—a bald, hilariously grotesque, bloated villain with more than a faint resemblance to Donald Pleasance, Dr. Strangelove and several late Marlon Brando performances. To play the part, Myers needed an elongated nose and ear as well as a padded suit, and had to spend two hours in makeup.

Dr. Evil is a relic from the 1950s who thinks there's too much loose living in the 1960s. Austin Powers, with his orange jacket and polka-dot shirt, is a walking illustration of everything Dr. Evil's against.

When Dr. Evil goes into a cryogenic sleep, Austin does the same. Thirty years later, they face off again in a much less freewheeling society. At that point, Austin, trying to thwart Dr. Evil's plan, is helped by Mrs. Kensington's daughter Vanessa—played by Elizabeth Hurley, whom Myers had in mind when he wrote the part. (He wanted someone who looked like those two sexpots of 1960s British popular culture, Julie Christie and Diana Rigg.)

Shooting the film was an unusually larky experience for Mike. But he had no idea whether there was a market for this movie. Might it be considered just an elaborate private joke?

"I created Austin Powers in memory of my father," Mike explained. "I had no idea if Austin would connect with modern audiences but I really didn't care at the time. I just wanted to do something I thought would have made my father laugh."

14

COMEBACK KID

*A*USTIN POWERS: *INTERNATIONAL MAN OF MYSTERY* seemed like
a private joke or just a funny valentine sent posthu-
mously from Mike Myers to his adored dad. Few
people—especially not the writer-star of the movie—
were expecting pandemonium at the box office for a
cheerful, scattershot romp about a British spy with
bad teeth, horn-rimmed glasses and a fondness for
velvet suits and lace shirts.

Indeed, no one was more surprised by the film's
success than those in the marketing department of
New Line Cinema. They were braced for the worst,

because audience response at test screenings had been mixed at best.

"We had a few screenings that went absolutely flat," Mike De Luca, at the time president of production for New Line, admitted to the *Los Angeles Times*.

In retrospect, it seemed apparent that New Line had been recruiting the wrong people for its test audience. Most of them sat there stony-faced. They didn't get it.

In the middle of one test screening, with both De Luca and Myers in attendance, the film broke, causing the audience to groan. Myers kept them from getting crankier by rushing to the front and entertaining people with 10 minutes of stand-up material until the film had been repaired.

The audience appreciated the interlude but still failed to love the movie.

"I think we found the only 900 people in America who didn't think the movie was funny," De Luca decided later.

What no one had realized was that *Austin Powers* would be embraced as a celebration, as well as a parody, of the wildest, nuttiest era in the history of popular culture. Thirty years on, the period could not only be laughed at for its excesses but also appreciated for its power to liberate the Western world from all the suffocating rules and regulations governing conventional behavior.

In the heyday of Austin Powers, men had only recently been freed from the necessity to wear ties and jackets, and to avoid strong colors unless they wanted to be considered as freakish as Liberace. Women were stuck with girdles and nylons, and it was definitely not OK for them to wear pants.

Even more revolutionary was the expansion of the definition of who could be considered sexually attractive. The biggest joke the movie had to offer was that you didn't have to look like Sean Connery in order to enjoy the sensually abundant lifestyle of James Bond. The hilarious miracle represented by Mike Myers as Austin Powers was that even if you were short and homely, with myopic vision, bad teeth and screamingly terrible taste in clothes, none of that need prevent you from being a successful hedonist and luring dozens of gorgeous women into your bed.

New Line executives felt both relieved and vindicated when *Austin Powers* morphed into one of Hollywood's key comedy phenomena of the 1990s. They weren't really prepared to cash in on it; there was no Austin Powers merchandise in the stores.

But Mike Myers was certainly ready to enjoy the benefits of the film's success. After four rather lean years, the career of the silly boy from Scarborough— which seemed to have reached its peak and then suddenly crashed in the early 1990s—was once more dramatically ascendant by the end of 1997.

At first, the staying power of *Austin Powers* was not apparent. The picture took in $54 million at the box office, which was excellent but not spectacular. Where it really showed its clout was at video stores some months after its theatrical run. On video the movie scored another $44 million—and made "Yeah, baby" and "Let's shag" into the public's favorite jocular phrases.

As Mike explained a couple of years later, he and his friend Jay Roach (later chosen to direct the movie) were just having a discussion. "We made it for ourselves," its writer and star insisted. "We never thought anybody else would like it. And now the irony is that Mike Myers is an employed actor."

As soon as Mike was back on top, he chose to take a huge risk. Instead of following the first Austin Powers movie with another broad comedy, he opted to play a serious role in a movie written and directed by the little-known Mark Christopher.

On May 26, 1997, *Variety* reported that Myers had signed to play Steve Rubell, the co-founder of Studio 54, the famous late 1970s and early 1980s New York disco on West 54th Street in Manhattan. The movie, called *54*, was to be a Miramax production.

Growing up in Dodge City, Iowa, in the 1970s, Christopher had read about Studio 54 in *After Dark* magazine and become intrigued. Later, after moving to New York to study film at Columbia University, he decided to write a script on the subject. He managed to get a Miramax executive interested, but he didn't want to sell the script unless he could direct it. At this point, Christopher had made only a few short films, but Miramax decided to give him a chance.

Mike explained why he was excited about getting a chance to play Rubell. "If the feeling in America in 1979 was that you were in the center of the universe, then Manhattan was the center of the center, Studio 54 was the center of the center of the center, and Steve Rubell was the center of the center of the center of the center. Here was this guy who had the world in the palm of his hand."

Beyond that, Myers felt a particular empathy for Rubell, partly because Mike and Steve were both guys who moved among the beautiful people while understanding at some basic level that they themselves were not pretty enough to make the cut.

"I just thought, 'My heart goes out to Steve Rubell,'" Myers told the *Los Angeles Times*. "Here's a guy who decided who was beautiful and interesting enough to get into his club, and yet he admitted that he would not have allowed himself into the club."

Consequently, Mike developed a clear case of disco fever. He was hardly the first comedy star to take a

serious role, but this was a first in his movie career. As
he explained, he had had serious roles on Canadian
television at the beginning of his career. He promised
he was not about to abandon comedy; he was trying
something a little different.

Twenty years after John Travolta's dancing in
Saturday Night Fever brought disco to Hollywood, it
was apparently time to revisit the feel-good pulse of
the dance floor in the days when people with leisure
suits and heavy eyeshadow decided to stop worrying
about the state of the world and just boogie.

The disco scene had its own culture and its own
value system. Sex and drugs were casually consumed
along the way; they went with the territory as naturally as popcorn and cola went with a Saturday night
at the movies. But discomania was short-lived; by the
mid-90s, moviemakers could present the disco era as a
period piece. It was time to get the party rolling again,
repackaged as nostalgia and cautionary melodrama.

In fact, *54* was not the only movie that would try to
revive the cocaine-sprinkled days when celebrities,
drug addicts, attention-seekers, models and hustlers
all turned up to catch the disco beat and enjoy the
hedonism of an era that was post-Pill and pre-AIDS.

At the same time that Mark Christopher was
making *54*, Whit Stillman, who had previously written
and directed *Metropolitan* and *Barcelona*, was working

on a movie called *The Last Days of Disco*—about a Manhattan dance club of the same era that was not actually called Studio 54 but had certain of its trademark accoutrements, such as its velvet ropes. Gramercy Pictures and Castle Rock were backing Stillman's movie.

At the real Studio 54, the party had screeched to a halt when the owners, Steve Rubell and Ian Schrager, pleaded guilty to evading corporate and personal taxes. Each served 13 months in prison.

They went bankrupt and the club was sold, but after getting out of jail, Rubell returned to Studio 54 as a consultant and tried to get the party going again. Unfortunately, things were never quite the same. Studio 54 closed in 1986. Three years later, Rubell died at age 45.

Why should there have been a resurgence of interest in Studio 54 more than a decade after its demise?

"People who are older want to look back," Mark Christopher explained to the *New York Times*, "and people who are younger want to see what it was like because it's so very different now."

Studio 54 was the symbol of a special epoch and a certain attitude. It had silver banquettes and spinning lights. It was the place where debutantes from the Upper East Side met wealthy visitors from Europe; where fashion models made out with rock stars; where artists would be photographed kissing socialites. It was a place where a handsome, well-built kid could be successfully on the make—just getting past the entrance and into the club was considered a mark of achievement.

Christopher saw the ritual of going to Studio 54 as if it were a trip to Oz. "To go through those doors, past those velvet ropes, you checked your life at the door. All your hangups were left behind. Anything could happen. The downside was that people didn't see where it was going. Ultimately the cost was jail for some, and drug addiction and AIDS for others."

Christopher chose to focus on a fictional working-class kid from New Jersey (played by Ryan Phillippe) who becomes a bartender at Studio 54.

That turned out to be a huge mistake, because it marginalized Myers, whose performance as Rubell was by far the most compelling thing about *54*. And the film's young protagonist was a rather bland and uninteresting Tom Cruise clone, whose trying-to-make-it-in-the-big-time story was numbingly familiar.

Much of the shooting was done in Mike Myers's hometown. A replica of Studio 54 was built on a Toronto soundstage.

Mike prepared for the role by taking on the look and style of Rubell—copying his hairstyle, his nose (with the help of prosthetics), his Brooklyn Jewish accent and his gestures. With all these affectations,

the danger was that the character would become a
male version of "Coffee Talk" host Linda Richman.
But somehow Myers avoided that trap. While working
on the film, he kept up that Brooklyn accent even on
his days off.

Making the film in Toronto, Mike found himself
surrounded by family and old friends. Occasionally,
this led to delicate problems. One day when Alice
wanted to visit the set to watch her famous son in
action, Mike had to suggest diplomatically that she
choose another day for her visit. He'd just as soon
she wasn't around when he had to come on to one of
the young waiters at Studio 54 with the line: "I'd like
to suck your cock."

But his impressive performance has a lot more to it
than shocking dialogue and an entertaining accent.
With a druggy, blissed-out smile, Myers catches the
pathetic desperation of this amiable, impulsive con
artist driven to associate with important people and
play court jester to the glitterati.

He's the somewhat screwed up yet mostly genial
lord of misrule to a large crowd of poseurs in polyester
leisure suits. And underneath it all, you can see that
this guy is just a scrambling amateur who got his start
by running a couple of steak houses in the suburbs. If
getting into Studio 54 is like taking a trip to Oz, then
Rubell, as played by Myers, is definitely reminiscent of

the supposedly great and powerful wizard who turns out to be just a cheap carny faker.

Myers also makes you understand how suicidal carelessness and a remarkable reliance on good luck seem to be part of Steve Rubell's personality. And so it doesn't seem at all improbable when Rubell, on a widely watched TV talk show, is asked about Studio 54's financial track record. In an almost willfully self-destructive gesture, he replies that what the IRS doesn't know won't hurt it. The result is a crackdown that ruins Rubell and his club.

Unfortunately, the movie can't quite make up its mind whether it's a celebration of the careless magic that drew people to Studio 54, or whether it's a shrill warning about the pitfalls of casual drugs and casual sex. And the more the movie concentrates on the escapades of its pretty young hero, the less we really care. We'd be much more likely to pay attention if the picture focused on Rubell.

From the point of view of Mike Myers, what this movie amounted to was an interesting failure, a change of pace for him, and an indication that, given the opportunity, this comedian was capable of doing extremely good work in a serious dramatic role.

When the movie was released in August 1998, it drew mostly dismissive reviews.

"Timid and meandering—a confused mishmash,"

said the *New York Times*.

"Flat and amateurish," said *Entertainment Weekly*.

Miramax boss Harvey Weinstein tried to make the picture's premiere as jolly as possible, praising everyone involved before the lights went down at Mann's Chinese theater in Hollywood.

The screening was followed by a glitzy disco event at a recreated Studio 54 on a Raleigh Studios sound stage.

Guests walked on a white carpet, and a giant disco ball hung over the bar. Myers attended the bash along with other stars of the picture as well as the director and producers. Celebrity guests included Lauren Holly, Lauren Hutton, Jon Lovitz, Sofia Coppola, Alan Carr, Nastassja Kinski and Marisa Berenson.

Despite all the hoopla, 54 vanished quickly from theaters.

Once it did, it was time for Mike Myers to get back to the business of being seriously funny.

15

SHAGADELIC

"So how do you get into those pants?"

"You could start by buying me a drink."

That's the opening exchange in the whacky court-ship of two secret agents in *Austin Powers: The Spy Who Shagged Me*, which opened in mid-June 1999 and immediately established itself as one of the biggest hits of the year.

As played by Heather Graham, Felicity Shagwell is a spoofy femme fatale, with her skin-tight, one-piece zippered outfit that ends in the shortest hot pants in cinematic history.

The object of her affection is, of course, that ultimate late-60s British nerd with a frilly ascot and countless other affectations.

The Spy Who Shagged Me starts with the hero's betrayal by his bride, Vanessa (an amusing cameo by Elizabeth Hurley), who is revealed during their honeymoon to be a robotic monster.

"Do you smoke after sex?" Vanessa inquires.

"I don't know," replies Austin. "I've never looked."

But when he takes a close look at Vanessa, he discovers that with the use of a remote control, she can be made to speak Spanish. This comes as a bit of a shock, but in the midst of their traumatic breakup, Austin realizes the good news: He is once more a bachelor on the lam.

Repeating one of the most reliable jokes from the first Austin Powers movie, our man with the thick lenses and snaggle teeth prances naked around his posh hotel. He grins and rolls his shoulders in a mood of triumphant liberation, wearing only a hairy chest pelt. As he marches through the lobby and down the stairs, various objects—including a child's toy and a baguette—keep interposing themselves between his private parts and the camera just in time. And his ass is covered, literally, by two sides of ham, as they're wheeled along on a serving cart.

It's the combination of Austin's shamelessly displayed

libido and his unsalvageable nerdiness that makes this spy masquerading as a fashion photographer a winningly funny hero.

In the second installment of the Austin Powers franchise, the plot centers on the possible destruction of Washington. Austin's mojo—his sex drive—has been stolen by his bald arch-enemy, Dr. Evil, also again played by Myers. This time, the cat-and-mouse game of Powers and Evil reverses the direction of their previous journey and carries them back to the 1960s, the age of paisley.

Mike Myers and director Jay Roach decided to give Dr Evil more screen time in the sequel. "Because Dr. Evil's journey was kind of undernourished in the first movie, we felt we could nourish it more in the second movie."

Austin gets the news from his intelligence boss, Basil Exposition (Michael York), that the world is again being imperiled by Dr. Evil, who has ended his exile in outer space. Thanks to a time machine, the villain has found his way back to the '60s—and he's demanding ransom.

At world domination headquarters, Dr. Evil has gathered his old team of troublemakers. There's Number Two (played as an older man by Robert Wagner while his younger self is portrayed by Rob Lowe, who has a marvelous knack for sending up

Wagner's mannerisms). Also back is the Teutonic scene-stealing sourpuss Frau Farbissina (Mindy Sterling).

Once again, Dr. Evil wears his trademark Nehru jacket, and Myers as Dr. Evil steals the movie from Myers as Austin. It seems Dr. Evil has a deadly weapon—a laser cannon stationed on the moon. But he's got an even more ingenious invention—a miniature clone dubbed Mini-Me, hilariously and wordlessly portrayed by Verne Troyer.

Mike got the idea for Mini-Me—a mute, thirty-two inch dwarf—while watching a video of an old Marlon Brando movie, *The Island of Dr. Moreau.*

Among Mini-Me's most endearing talents is his ability to mimic all of Dr. Evil's gestures—such as his way of forming mock quotation marks with his fingers. Somewhat less lovable is his habit of terrorizing his colleagues by biting them.

According to Myers, Verne Troyer was an inspiration to everyone who worked with him. "He's all about what you can do and not what you can't do," he explained. "He drives his own car, he's self-sufficient, he never complains. He's spent a lifetime of people saying things like, 'What a cute LITTLE coat.' But he's come to some sort of peace with it."

The arrival of Mini-Me prompts a deliciously funny Freudian battle between Dr. Evil and his estranged real son, Scott Evil (played by Seth Green, repeating his role from the first film). When Scott attempts a reconciliation with his father, the old man snarls: "You had your chance. I already have someone created in my image. He's evil, he wants to take over the world, and he fits easily into most overhead storage bins."

And, oh yes, unlike Scott, Mini-Me doesn't whine, and he doesn't talk back.

Unfortunately, instead of stopping while he was ahead, Myers took on a third role in this movie—the hugely unfunny villain Fat Bastard.

Fat Bastard is an obese, revolting lout with a thick Scottish accent. The joke here is that he considers himself incredibly sexy. But it's not enough of a joke. The character is nasty and repulsive without being witty. And there doesn't seem to be much point to the exercise except as a demonstration of the star's ability to play diverse roles and put up with mammoth discomfort and three hours in the makeup chair to make himself disappear into Fat Bastard's blubber.

Apart from the sour note introduced by Fat Bastard, the movie is a cheerful if thin pastiche of everything you ever enjoyed about swinging London—the James Bond movies, the Beatles, *Blow-Up*, the mod fashions of Carnaby Street. Also thrown into the mix: plenty of toilet humor, predictable jokes about *Star Wars*, and set pieces, such as an extended sight gag in which

Felicity, viewed in silhouette, appears to be extracting an umbrella and other large objects from Austin's derrière.

Other diversions include cameo appearances by Woody Harrelson and Willie Nelson, and a special appearance by Burt Bacharach and Elvis Costello doing a musical number in a swinging London locale. A much funnier musical interlude comes when Dr. Evil and Mini-Me do a hip-hop version of "The Two of Us."

Myers and Roach worked out a loose way of shooting so that parts of the dialogue could be improvised.

In the funniest exchange, Dr. Evil tells Frau Farbissina, who has turned into his lover: "I can't let my feelings for you interfere with my taking over the world."

At one point when Austin questions the time-travel logic of the plot, his boss, Basil Exposition, retorts: "I suggest you don't worry about this sort of thing, and just enjoy yourself."

Then, turning to the camera, he says: "That goes for the rest of you, too."

For the most part, the audience seemed willing to go along with that advice.

The critics, however, weren't so sure.

"Bigger isn't necessarily better," said *Variety*, adding that it feels like a quickie.

In the *New York Times*, Janet Maslin said: "The sequel is several love beads short of its predecessor, but some of that was bound to happen once Austin's novelty dimmed."

David Denby of the *New Yorker* put it this way: "The two Austin Powers movies could only be called crud classics. We call them classics grudgingly and with a certain loss of self-respect."

The blatant emphasis on commercial exploitation of its own success raised the question of whether Myers might have turned into what he had started out satirizing.

In *Wayne's World*, seven years earlier, Myers had made a mockery of product placement. Now, in *The Spy Who Shagged Me*, he was taking commercial exploitation to new levels even by Hollywood standards. The movie opened on more than 3,000 screens on June 11, 1999. And this time, New Line Cinema was not caught off guard the way it had been when the first Austin Powers movie had opened two years earlier.

The production budget for *Austin Powers: The Spy Who Shagged Me* was $33 million (U.S.), close to double that of the first Austin Powers movie. But even more dramatic was the contrast between the way the films were marketed.

When *Austin Powers: International Man of Mystery* became a surprise hit in 1997, consumers actually complained that there was no Austin Powers merchandise available for sale. That mistake would not be repeated.

In the summer of 1999, the selling of Austin Powers became the merchandising sensation of the season. First of all, New Line itself was spending more on promoting the movie (close to $40 million U.S.) than it did on making the picture.

And every detail was plotted with the precision of a military strike. That included the selection of the opening date—three weeks after the premiere of the year's most eagerly awaited blockbuster—the *Star Wars* prequel, *The Phantom Menace*. The theory was that *Austin Powers* would pop up just when the public was getting tired of *The Phantom Menace*.

Even before *Austin Powers* had been shot, New Line cleverly played its *Star Wars* card in a commercial dropped into the Super Bowl telecast in January. "If you see only one movie this summer, see *Star Wars*," went the cheeky tag line. "But if you see two movies, see *Austin Powers: The Spy Who Shagged Me*."

New Line took advantage of the fact that it is owned by Time Warner to exploit its corporate synergy. There were tie-in products from Warner Records and Warner Books. Meanwhile HBO made plans to produce an Austin Powers cartoon series. And the film was promoted by *Entertainment Weekly*,

Time, and the two Turner TV networks, TNT and TBS.

Meanwhile, major companies lined up to get in on the action. Everyone wanted to be associated with Austin Powers; it was a way to show your outfit was hip, cool and groovy.

Sample One: "When you transfer a balance, the Austin Powers Titanium Visa card gives you a low, money-save introductory rate, followed by a low, 10.99% interest rate—an offer that just may inspire you to say 'Yeah, baby, yeah!'"

Sample Two: "The smashing all-new 2000 Mitsubishi Eclipse, which swings into dealerships in July, will experience a little cross-mojonation as cats and kittens . . . can build their own Eclipse spy-cars worthy of Britain's swinging secret agent, Austin Powers. Oh, behave!"

Then there were the product placements, including Heineken Beer and Virgin Atlantic Airlines, which temporarily nicknamed itself Virgin Shaglantic.

And what did Dr. Evil choose for his new head-quarters? The Starbucks Coffee Company.

"Naturally, we were a little concerned being associated with Dr. Evil," a Starbucks spokesman told Michael Colton of the business magazine *Brill's Content*. "But we've never been a company afraid to laugh at ourselves."

No payment was involved for this product placement.

Merchandise on sale while the film was in theaters included action figures, inflatable furniture, a new version of the board game Clue, a talking watch and a penis-enlarger. And there was a talking doll based on the most popular new character introduced in the sequel, Mini-Me.

In certain parts of the U.S., Toys'R'Us received complaints from customers offended by a talking Austin Powers doll that said, "Do I make you horny, baby, do I?"

The frenzy of cross-promotion certainly paid off in terms of the movie's performance at the box office. In its first weekend alone, *The Spy Who Shagged Me* knocked *The Phantom Menace* out of first place and took in $57 million (U.S.)—more than the original Austin Powers had grossed in its entire theatrical life. It went on to become one of the top-grossing movie comedies ever made, raking in close to $200 million (U.S.).

In case there was any doubt that Mike Myers had made a sensational comeback after being written off as a has-been in 1993, the huge success of this movie removed it. He was now in a position to choose his own projects—with studios lining up for the privilege of paying him preposterous amounts of money.

Still, Mike claimed it didn't make all that much difference.

Just before the movie opened, he remarked: "I'm out of the 'It's-gotta-be-a-big hit' business, because it doesn't mean anything. When a movie is a big hit, it doesn't solve any of your personal problems. It doesn't answer any of your universal questions like 'What the hell are we doing on this planet?' I mean, it's nice, but it's not the full picture."

16

DIETERGATE

THE SPY WHO SHAGGED ME was not the only movie release of 1999 directed by Jay Roach with Mike Myers in the cast. The other one was Disney's *Mystery, Alaska*. The script was by David E. Kelley, the hugely successful creator of *Ally McBeal*, *Picket Fences* and other TV series. It had been pitched as a cross between *Slapshot*, the Paul Newman hockey movie, and *Northern Exposure*, the prestigious TV series. It was on the basis of his success with *Austin Powers: International Man of Mystery* that Roach got a deal with Disney.

The storyline pits an NHL team, the New York Rangers, against a gang of rowdy amateurs. The premise is that the inhabitants of a remote town are so obsessed with hockey that they leave their streets frozen so they can skate down them. Usually, they play on the town pond, but they're so good at the game that they are challenged to play an exhibition game against the Rangers.

The four lead actors: Burt Reynolds, Russell Crowe, Ron Eldard and Hank Azaria. The town chosen for the shoot: Canmore, Alberta.

Jay Roach knew next to nothing about hockey, but he had a friend who was a hockey fanatic: Mike Myers. In fact, Myers had given him a pair of skates as a present. And, of course, Roach wanted something else from Mike: He wanted him to be in this movie.

Myers does an amusing fast cameo as a sports commentator, but it's not enough to lift *Mystery, Alaska* out of its doldrums. The reviewers dismissed it as a rather mild-mannered movie that gets bogged down in too many plot points. And when it was released in October 1999, just four months after the premiere of *The Spy Who Shagged Me*, it disappeared from theaters quickly.

The result: Jay Roach, whose only big success was tied up with *Austin Powers*, had tried to break out on his own—and flopped.

In the meantime, Mike had made a serious commitment to the first major new comedy project he would write and star in since 1993 without Roach's collaboration.

News of it first surfaced in June 1998, when *Variety* reported that Imagine Entertainment (co-owned by Ron Howard and Brian Grazer) would produce *Sprockets*, featuring Dieter, one of the most inventive and popular of the characters from Mike's days on *Saturday Night Live*.

In fact, the character—a terribly solemn German talk-show host—predates Myers's arrival at *SNL*. It was developed in the late 1980s while Myers was still in Toronto, and was inspired by a waiter he used to hang out with.

Brian Grazer had been courting Myers for some time. In early 1998, they had a meeting arranged by Myers's manager at that time. Mike suggested a movie about Dieter. Grazer jumped at the idea. Grazer was confident he could sell it to Universal, since Imagine was the studio's biggest and most reliable supplier of product.

In April 1998, Universal made a deal that called for a $10-million payment to Myers. Within a year, he was to turn in a first-draft screenplay. Imagine was bullish on the project, even though other movies spun off from *Saturday Night Live* sketches had tanked—the

first *Wayne's World* movie being an exception to the
rule.

By mid-1999, Imagine and Universal were congrat-
ulating themselves on their brilliant foresight. After
all, *Austin Powers: The Spy Who Shagged Me* had just
become the second-biggest hit of the season. But with
the success of the movie, they had to keep pushing up
the fee for Myers to match his escalating market price.
Eventually, his *Dieter* fee reached $21.5 million (U.S.).
But there was another issue besides money that
needed to be resolved.

In August 1999, two months after the release of
Austin Powers: The Spy Who Shagged Me, Universal
Studios and Imagine Entertainment announced that
Myers had officially signed for *Sprockets* and one other
unnamed film.

Universal was determined to have a big hit on thousands of screens for the summer of 2001, and the
studio was under a lot of pressure. Universal was
owned by the Seagram Company Ltd., and Edgar
Bronfman, CEO of Seagram, had made a deal to
merge his empire with the French conglomerate
Vivendi. As a result, sweeping corporate changes were
anticipated, setting off waves of fear. Top executives,
including Universal Studios president Ron Meyer,
were anxiously trying to hang on to their jobs. They
needed to demonstrate they could produce hits, and

they also needed to demonstrate they could play hard-ball with temperamental, creative people. The result would be an unprecedented outbreak of warfare between a studio and a movie star—a shocking affair that became known in the industry as Dietergate.

Mike worked relentlessly and obsessively on the script, but he was never satisfied with it. He worked first with co-writer Jack Handley, then with Mike McCullers. And he talked to people at the Imagine office as often as twice a day about various details.

The plot: Dieter, movie critic and existentialist talk-show host, faces a crisis. His beloved pet has been monkey-napped. Dieter must travel to the United States to rescue it. Part of the concept: The early sequences in Germany are filmed in severe black and white. When Dieter arrives in Los Angeles, the movie bursts into color—the way *The Wizard of Oz* did when Dorothy left Kansas and landed in Oz.

Imagine and Universal assured themselves that even though there seemed to be an endless series of small irritations and glitches concerning *Dieter*, things would work out well. The script, they thought, was getting better and better. They were sure it was going to be a hit—and any problem that came up they regarded as a minor detail. They weren't picking up clues from Mike that he wasn't feeling nearly as buoyant about *Dieter* as they were.

But members of Mike's own circle of friends and advisers were well aware of his increasing worries. He tested some of the material at the Groundlings comedy club on Melrose Avenue, and things did not go well. Then, in late May, he brought a group of friends together for a reading. The response confirmed his doubts. There were brilliant bits, there were hilarious gags, but he had not been able to flesh out the character enough. The heart of the movie just wasn't there.

Myers felt he had creative control and script approval, but he was getting nervous about the August 14 date that Universal and Imagine had set for the start of principal photography. And there was a reason for his nervousness. He had once before been in the odd situation of trying to come back with another winner after scoring a huge hit. He remembered how it felt back in 1992, when expectations were huge after his first *Wayne's World* movie. In the end, that hit seemed like a set-up for a huge fall, which followed a year later with the back-to-back flops *So I Married an Axe Murderer* and *Wayne's World 2*.

The result had been a horrible meltdown, one of the most devastating periods of Mike's life. Now, after two phenomenally popular Austin Powers movies, he had to be wondering: Was he letting himself walk into another ambush?

Myers had escalated his salary from $10 million to more than $20 million for *Dieter* based on the take of *The Spy Who Shagged Me*. But money wasn't the big issue for him. What really scared him was that the picture might not be funny enough. He was being spooked again by his ultimate fear: that he would be found out and arrested by the no-talent police.

There were times in the past when Mike had felt a similar instinct to call a halt. It had happened with the second *Wayne's World* movie. Mike felt the script wasn't ready, and he didn't want to go ahead with it. But he'd allowed himself to be bullied, and he wound up making the movie. In retrospect, he had to wonder whether he should have stood his ground. This time, he wasn't going to give in so easily.

The fact was, plans for the making of *Dieter* were hurtling ahead at an alarming rate. Production designer Bo Welch *(Men in Black)* had been signed to direct his first feature. David Hasselhoff, of the cult-favorite TV series *Baywatch*, had been cast as the villain who steals Dieter's beloved monkey. And Jack Black, who had received rave reviews for his performance as an opinionated record-store owner in *High Fidelity*, was signed to play Dieter's sidekick.

The top executives at Universal and Imagine didn't grasp the situation until the end of May. Returning to work after the Memorial Day long weekend, they received urgent demands from Mike Myers. It was absolutely essential, he said, to have an emergency summit meeting about *Dieter*.

At the meeting, which took place in the 14th-floor office of Universal Studios' president Ron Meyer, few realized what bomb was about to be dropped. It wasn't just that there were more little problems that had to be solved. This time, their $21.5-million star and writer had come to tell them they had to call a halt. *Dieter* just wasn't ready to be made. Mike had script approval, and he didn't approve of the script.

To the executives, this seemed like a catch-22 absurdity. Myers was the script writer, so if as the star he didn't approve of the script, all he had to do was fix it. But, according to Mike, he had tried everything, and *Dieter* couldn't be fixed.

The message Myers was sending was: He couldn't solve the script problem in time to start filming August 14. He needed to put the script away for a while and come back to it later. If Universal needed a movie, he would do something else—but not *Dieter*, not yet.

The meeting went on for more than an hour, with Universal executives trying to persuade Mike that he was overreacting to the problem. If the script needed polishing or doctoring, they would bring in the best and highest-paid writers in the business.

The next day, a Universal lawyer sent a stiff letter accusing Myers of abandoning the project in midstream in breach of his legally binding commitments. According to the letter, Universal had already spent $3.8 million on the project. Myers had his lawyer send a stinging rebuttal, arguing that Myers had never approved the script, and accusing Universal of steamrolling ahead and engaging in fraud.

By this point, the gloves were definitely off. A flurry of phone calls failed to resolve the problem.

On June 7, *E! Online* reported that Universal had filed a lawsuit against the comedian in Los Angeles Superior Court. Seeking $5 million, Universal claimed Myers had a binding contract and must not be allowed to work on other projects until this commitment was honored.

Myers issued a statement: "I cannot in good conscience accept $20 million and cheat moviegoers who pay their hard-earned money to see my work. My agreement with Universal has always been that the movie would not be made until I approved the script. I informed Universal that the script does not work, and it needs more time to be fixed."

Universal also issued a statement: "We are living up to our end of the deal and expect Mr. Myers to live up to his end. We are filing this lawsuit to enforce our rights."

A week later, Universal shut down the production, which was costing about $200,000 a week to keep afloat. The studio blamed Myers for the fact that 25 employees were thrown out of work. Stacy Snider, chairman of Universal, said: "While we are extremely disappointed that we are not able to make this film, we are particularly anguished when considering all the talented individuals who came on board based on Mike Myers's commitment to this project, and as a result, gave up other opportunities in order to do this film."

The dispute got even uglier on July 7, when Myers was hit with a second lawsuit, this time from Imagine Entertainment. Seeking $30 million in damages, Imagine claimed the script issue was just a smokescreen.

Imagine's over-the-top statement of claim made Myers sound like one of the worst tyrants in history. "He has followed a pattern and practice of breaking his promises, betraying the trust of others, and causing serious damages to those with whom he deals through selfish, egomaniacal and irresponsible conduct," it charged.

And Imagine's attorney, Bert Fields, made no secret of his own rage. "In my view," he remarked, "it's about time somebody stood up to this guy. I think the jury and the public will be stunned when they hear the things he said and did."

To which Martin Singer, representing Myers, retorted: "The claims made by Imagine are fictional and without merit."

A few days later, Mike fired back, filing a $20-million countersuit against Universal Pictures. Among the accusations: fraud and deceit, invasion of privacy and defamation.

In his claim, Myers stated that Universal and Imagine executives had argued that the *Dieter* script was "good enough," and that with the comedian's huge box-office draw, they would all stand to make large amounts of money if he would just go through with the movie.

Myers also alleged that Imagine partner Ron Howard told him things were going to get ugly if he didn't agree to make the film.

Robin Ruzan was named as a plaintiff along with her husband in the lawsuit. The couple claimed a process server hired by Universal stalked them while attempting to serve the papers—and chased them down unlit, winding streets. The result, they claimed, was a serious invasion of privacy that might force them to move. Myers and Ruzan blamed Grazer for deliberately giving the process server their home address rather than the business address of their attorney, Martin Singer.

Speaking to trade press reporters, Imagine attorney Bert Fields mocked Myers for this statement. "Myers must really be getting desperate," he said. "He's flailing around in all directions now."

By now, all of Hollywood was in an uproar over the case. Something had to be done about this. It was not only damaging to both sides, it was damaging to the entire industry.

Emerging as the Henry Kissinger peacemaker: Jeffrey Katzenberg, one of the three principals at DreamWorks SKG. Katzenberg had been a partner at the new company for several years, along with Steven Spielberg and David Geffen.

Because of his many years at Disney as second-in-command to Michael Eisner, Katzenberg was Hollywood's king of animation movies. And there was a very specific reason why DreamWorks had a stake in this dispute. Set to be released in the spring of 2001 was a cartoon movie called *Shrek*, masterminded by Kaztzenberg and featuring the voice of Mike Myers as the title character.

With the help of Spielberg and his strong ties with Universal, Katzenberg emerged as the fixer who could rise above the fray, acting as a buffer between Myers on one side and Universal and Imagine on the other.

Even so, according to Greg Kilday of the *Los Angeles Times*, the deal took two weeks to hammer out, almost coming apart several times. Finally, a settlement was announced in the second week of August.

In the end, *Dieter* was dropped. So were the lawsuits on both sides. Myers agreed to make up for *Dieter* by developing a new character for a movie that would be made through a collaboration involving Universal, DreamWorks and Imagine. Mike would be spared having to deal creatively with either Imagine or Universal. The movie would be distributed in North America by Universal and abroad by DreamWorks.

"There's been a good deal of emotion," Katzenberg remarked in a striking understatement. "Ultimately the business stuff always gets resolved. What lingers on for a while are the hurt feelings."

There was more truth to that than Katzenberg perhaps realized at the time. Dietergate was far from over.

17

UNDER SIEGE

SETTLING THE DIETER LAWSUITS in August 2000 was a big relief for Mike Myers, but legal issues and the financial mess represented only part of his problem. An even greater concern, which could not be so neatly resolved, was the horrendous deluge of negative press Myers had received.

One of the nastiest examples was a column by Peter Bart, editor of *Variety*, which carried the headline "Mike Gets Mired." Written in the form of a memo, it was a lecture about ethics from a famous Hollywood journalist whose own ethics would come under scrutiny a year later, resulting in his suspension from his job.

Here is how it began:

"As the man who created Austin Powers, Mike, you aren't exactly a bundle of laughs of late. You've been backing out of movies, suing studios, hurling charges at industry icons. Perhaps most important, you've broken the code. Comedians just don't go around breaking the code, Mike. Especially polite Canadian comedians."

It went on in this scolding tone: "You don't seem to play by the rules, Mike—hence the sudden flurry of litigation involving you, Universal and Imagine."

More than once in this column, Bart used Mike's Canadian origins against him, ending with the threat that if he didn't mend his ways, he could be kicked out of the United States and sent back to dreaded Canada.

According to Bart, one of the most heinous things Myers had done was to compare himself to John Lennon.

"Let me remind you of a key distinction, Mike," Bart cautioned Myers. "John Lennon was a legend. You're still a comic with a green card. A talented comic, to be sure. I'd hate to see you end up back in Toronto, recycling hoser jokes."

It's hard to say what was most offensive about Bart's attack—his condescension to Myers, his contempt for all things Canadian or his toadying to the Hollywood studio establishment.

Unfortunately, Bart's attack on Myers was not an isolated case. The dust-up over Dieter came along during the dog days of summer when the media were desperate for material, and the ongoing lawsuits provided a gripping drama with big names, a power struggle and an episodic structure. Reputations, strong emotions and a lot of money were on the line. The showbiz press couldn't get enough of it.

But Bart's column was child's play compared with the nuclear attack about to be launched by *Vanity Fair* magazine.

Written by Kim Masters—best known for her book about Disney—the article was called "Ganging Up on Mike." It opened with a breathless account of the night that boxers Oscar de la Hoya and Shane Mosley squared off at an arena in downtown Los Angeles.

At the arena that night, Brian Grazer, one of the Imagine Entertainment partners suing Myers, ran into Jeffrey Katzenberg and Steven Spielberg of DreamWorks. It took him a few minutes to notice that Mike Myers and his wife, Robin Ruzan, were part of the same group, but he decided to be polite nevertheless. And then—this is the shocking part—instead of being warm and friendly, Myers stared at him coldly and barely returned his handshake. And Robin wouldn't even shake his hand.

So just what did Kim Masters think Brian Grazer was expecting? Hugs and kisses?

Masters segues from this incident into a damning indictment of Myers. The fight between de la Hoya and Mosley, she explains, was tame stuff compared with the battle between Myers (in one corner) and Universal and Imagine (in the other). And then, she makes this devastating connection: "Some in the long line of agents, lawyers, managers, executives, and film-makers who have been in ruptured relationships with Myers saw the whole ugly episode as proof the exis-tence of a higher power."

What is the basis of this demonization? Apparently, Masters discovered, there were some days on some movie sets when Mike Myers wasn't always a treat to be with. There were even times when he could be petty enough to complain about the selection of lunch meats or the unavailability of margarine. This must have come as a shock to those who'd previously thought that comedians were all joke-cracking, happy-go-lucky folk, and that movie stars, as a rule, were the nicest, least-demanding people you could ever meet.

It seemed more than slightly ironic that this notori-ous hatchet job should come from the very magazine that had made its reputation and its fortune largely by combining glamorous style with a preposterously sycophantic approach to movie stars and other Hollywood power mongers. For a typical feature story, *Vanity Fair* often goes so far as to allow publicists to set the conditions under which movie stars deign to appear on the magazine's cover.

Masters made much of the fact that Myers had hired private investigator Anthony Pellicano, who was famous for helping celebrity clients dig up dirt on their adversaries.

With no indication that she might be kidding, Masters even accused Myers of firing a manager after discovering the guy was on a plane to New York when Myers wanted him in Los Angeles. According to Masters, Myers wanted the manager to have the plane turned around—and when that didn't happen, he took extreme measures. Did Masters seriously expect readers to assume that Mike believed his manager had the power to have a plane turned around?

One of the few people quoted in defence of Myers was Lorne Michaels, creator of *Saturday Night Live*. "I know you can make a really strong case against Mike because he has clearly frustrated and angered so many people," Michaels admitted. "But I also think that it's not coming from any place of malice, and that he only cares about getting it right. People who want to get things off their desk shouldn't work with Mike Myers."

Perhaps the most damning section of the *Vanity Fair* article concerned Dana Andersen, an old colleague of Myers from his days at Second City's Toronto mainstage in the late 1980s.

Andersen told Masters that the inspiration for the Dieter character had come from him, and that Myers had never given him credit for it. Andersen, still working in relative obscurity in comedy cabaret theater in Edmonton, claimed he'd been the first one to utter the phrase "Touch my monkey."

Andersen told Masters he had developed a character named Kurt, who was a German avant-garde perform-ance artist. The way Andersen remembered it, Myers asked to join the sketch playing Kurt's sidekick. That, Andersen insisted, was how Dieter was born.

Mike, however, had a different version of history: He had created the character of Dieter and then invited Andersen to join the sketch as Dieter's lover, Kurt. Myers claims the character of Dieter was based on various sources, including a German exchange student he had met, and a waiter in Toronto who was given to making odd pronouncements, such as "I love textures. I would love to touch a monkey sometime."

What really rankled Andersen was that after Myers became famous, he seemed to forget he had ever known Dana Andersen. When Dieter became a huge success on *Saturday Night Live*, Andersen told

Masters, Myers failed to give him any credit—or even to invite him to visit the set or the join the audience at *SNL*.

In early August, only a month or so before the October 2000 issue of *Vanity Fair* was set to hit the stands with Masters's muckraking piece, the warring factions reached an agreement and tried to put Dietergate behind them. But, of course, it was in the magazine's interest to suggest this was not really the end of the affair.

"The battle ended, but it lit a bonfire of anger and resentment that's still burning," said *Vanity Fair*. Actually, it was the *Vanity Fair* article that ensured the Dietergate nightmare of Mike Myers would not go away.

Mike was extremely upset by the article, and he began making phone calls to friends and colleagues from the past, trying to repair or limit the damage. Among those who received such a call was Linda Kash, who'd been with Myers both in the touring company of Second City and then at the Toronto mainstage.

According to an article in the *Toronto Sun* by Jim Slotek, Kash was among several former Myers colleagues in Toronto who had issues with him. It was not Kash but her friend the comedy director Bruce Hunter who told Slotek that while filming *So I Married an Axe Murderer*, Myers had co-opted a line created by Kash years before, when they were working together at Second City. The joke, based on Kash's personal experience, was about a girl who explained the reason she'd dumped her boyfriend was that he smelled like soup.

By the early 1990s, Kash had moved to Los Angeles and had actually tried out for a part in *Axe Murderer* (which she didn't get). When Myers asked if it was all right to use her old joke, she was stunned to hear the scene had already been filmed. Though she was broke at the time, nobody offered her money for this contribution.

Slotek's article quoted Joe Bodolai, one of the producers of the short-lived CBC show *It's Only Rock 'n' Roll*, on which Wayne Campbell and Dieter both appeared years before they reached a larger audience on *Saturday Night Live*.

"I'm disappointed with Mike," Bodolai told Slotek. "I think all Dana [Andersen] or anyone ever wanted was for him to call and say 'Hi' and maybe just be recognized for what we did to help him."

In his early days in Toronto, Bodolai recalled, Mike always used to say that he never wanted to wind up as "a show-business fuck." So as a joke, one of Bodolai's colleagues on the TV show once took a Polaroid photo of Myers and wrote "Show-business fuck" on it.

"I still have the Polaroid," Bodolai told Slotek. "I'd love to send it to him."

Linda Kash was more forgiving. When Myers got back in touch with her in the wake of Dietergate to apologize and make sure she wasn't still mad about the long-ago incident (his use of her joke about the boyfriend who smelled like soup), Kash appreciated the gesture of the phone call from Myers. She told him it was OK, she felt sorry he was being pilloried, and she wished him well.

But the most dramatic reconciliation of all came when Mike took Edmonton by surprise with a whirl-wind 24-hour visit so he could make amends with Dana Andersen. After the *Vanity Fair* article came out, Myers phoned Andersen, hoping to patch up their quarrel over the origins of Dieter. At the end of a lengthy conversation, Andersen asked Myers if he'd be willing to come to Edmonton to guest star in the season's opening for *Die-Nasty*, the Alberta capital's long-running improvised soap opera.

And so it came to pass, to the delight of the audience on opening night, the first Monday in October 2000, that Mike Myers bounded on stage at Old Strathcona's Varscona Theatre playing a character he'd made famous on *Saturday Night Live*—a sheep-loving Celtic chieftain named Llchhwchh, who feels inadequate.

Wearing a kilt, fur vest and Viking helmet, Myers
delighted the crowd—and cracked up a couple of his
fellow performers. Applying for a job, his character
explains his credentials: "I can't read or write, but I
like to have sex with animals."

Though Mike had confirmed several times he was
coming, the producers didn't feel sure he was going to
show up—until they heard a knock at the back door at
7:45 P.M., 15 minutes before curtain. Myers immediately went down to the costume room and grabbed a
skirt to wear in the opening scene.

After the show, Mike joined the cast of 10 at the
Elephant and Castle pub. He spent the night at the
Macdonald Hotel. Before flying home the next day, he
visited another old friend, comedienne Sandra
Shamas, and took a quick tour of the Citadel,
Edmonton's most architecturally notable theater.

Throughout the fall, Mike was in recovery mode.
That summer he had bought a small house in midtown Toronto on Boswell Avenue, hoping to spend
more time in his hometown. According to its previous
owner, TV writer-director Ken Finkleman, the house
is amazingly easy to maintain, and it has the advantage
of being right downtown, close to everything.

"It's like a hotel room," said Finkleman. "You could
just drop your bags." Indeed, the house was only a few
blocks from the Four Seasons Yorkville hotel, where

Myers usually stays in Toronto, and his favorite pub, the Duke of York on Prince Arthur Avenue.

In October, Mike and Robin got into a bidding war and paid more than $2 million (U.S.) for a secluded Cape Cod–style house in Beverly Hills. (It even had gates to make them feel safe from aggressive process servers.)

And in December, Myers said a tentative yes to fellow-Canadian Ivan Reitman, who had been wooing him to play the Peter Sellers role in a remake of *The Pink Panther*. Reitman had assured him he could collaborate on the script. Sellers was one of Mike Myers's boyhood idols, and Sellers in *The Pink Panther* had been Eric Myers's idea of sheer comic bliss. But a few months later, Myers withdrew from the project. He was deeply honored to be asked, he said. But he was already playing one famous bumbler, Austin Powers. Two big-time bumblers would be one too many.

18

THE HAPPY OGRE

I<small>N THE WAKE OF</small> <small>DIETERGATE</small>, the last thing Mike
Myers needed was another controversy, but he walked
right into one at the Academy Awards presentation on
March 25, 2001.

All eyes that night were on Julia Roberts, considered a sure-thing winner for *Erin Brockovitch*. Myers
had the relatively low-key task of presenting the
Oscars for best sound and best sound editing.

Not wishing to come across as too bland and
boring, he balked at the script he was asked to deliver
and tried to liven up the proceeding with a joke. He

forgot that the Academy can be stunningly humorless when certain raw nerves are touched.

Before presenting the awards, Mike remarked: "Now, ladies and gentlemen, the award we've all been waiting for . . . Julia! OK, sound and sound editing. Now, I know what you're asking youself. Will the winner this year be Chet Flippy or Tommy Blub-Blub? . . . We don't know, but what I do know is that what's in this envelope is gonna send shock waves through the industry. Oh, yeah!"

The award for sound went to Scott Millan, Bob Beemer and Ken Weston for *Gladiator*. Jon Johnson took the award for best sound editing for *U-571*.

The day after the show, Robert Rehme, president of the Academy of Motion Picture Arts and Sciences, received a complaint from Donald C. Rogers, chairman of the executive committee of the Academy's sound branch.

"The comments made by Mike Myers during the presentation were at the very least offensive," Rogers wrote, "but greater than that, an insult to what we all know the film industry to be—a combination of wonderful sights and sounds. There is no excuse for demeaning the hard work of any individual on a project, ever. What makes this even more insulting is that the insult was delivered as an introduction to the award."

According to Rogers, getting a nomination is for many people the culmination of a career. "Their families are watching, and it's a moment of great pride for all associated with the project. Being publicly humiliated for having an unrecognizable name . . . removed all the joy of the event, and was embarrassing to say the least. I spoke to one individual who asked, 'How could the Academy do this to us?'"

Rogers demanded to know whether Myers's remarks had been written into the script, and if so, why they were approved.

Rehme wrote back: "I'm told that Mr. Myers was largely responsible for the content of his introduction, but that this wasn't a case of an onstage ad lib; his remarks were on the teleprompter. We will certainly endeavour to see that it doesn't happen again, although as we've seen, it's difficult to control every word of the script."

The producer of the Oscar show, Gil Cates, confessed that he had approved the comedian's remarks, which Myers had written himself.

"I thought it was amusing," said Cates (who had left for a vacation in Hawaii after the show) in a phone interview with the *Los Angeles Times*. "I didn't mean it to cause any harm. I'm sorry if it did. I wouldn't have used it if I had known it would come across the way it did. Myers thought it would be funny, and I thought it would, too, and I was wrong.

"Certainly Mike Myers intended no discourtesy. He's a wonderful guy who has been a presenter on the show several times. He's a very decent fellow and just a joy in terms of trying to be lighthearted. He meant no discourtesy, nor did I."

Robert Rehme and Bruce Davis, the Academy's exeutive director, blamed themselves for failing to flag the potential problem.

"Mike Myers is not the villain here," said Davis. "I have no idea how this came about, but every presenter is special. Those who are comedians are looking for ways to punch up their introductory remarks. Not all of them think it through as carefully as they might."

Rehme added: "It's our fault. Mike Myers is a charming guy. He would do anything we asked him to do. This just slipped through."

During the whole uproar, Myers was conspicuously unavailable for comment. In fact, he had been remarkably unavailable for any interviews since Dietergate. One reason: As part of the settlement of the lawsuits, Myers was under gag orders, and had to go through a complex set of procedures before being allowed to talk to the media.

Another reason: Jeffrey Katzenberg, the man who had extricated Myers from the *Dieter* mess, wanted Myers to be low-profile until the release in May of

Shrek. That way, Katzenberg hoped to maximize the impact of Mike's promotional efforts for the film—a much-touted DreamWorks cartoon movie with Myers as the voice of the title character.

That spring, Mike spent quite a lot of time in Toronto. Besides appearing on an April Fool's Day panel about comedy at a benefit for Humber College's comedy program, he came to town several times to cheer his beloved Toronto Maple Leafs during the Stanley Cup hockey playoffs.

By this time, Myers had sold his house on Boswell Avenue. He had owned it for less than a year and spent only a few nights in it.

Ironically, considering Mike's devotion to the Maple Leafs, the man who bought the house (without being aware of who was selling it) was Maple Leafs player Cory Cross.

No matter how successful he became, and despite the pull of Los Angeles, Mike remained as devoted to the Toronto Maple Leafs as when he was in high school. One night when he was in Toronto for a playoff game, Mike was supposed to be taken by limousine from Yorkville to the Air Canada Centre downtown, where the game was being played. But rather than fight traffic, he decided it would be faster to take the subway. Rush-hour travelers on the Toronto transit system were startled that evening

when, at the busy St. George subway station, they
found themselves walking past a hockey fan who bore
a striking resemblance to Austin Powers.

A week later, Mike found himself at the Cannes
Film Festival for the world premiere of *Shrek*. The
picture, which immediately after its premiere opened
on thousands of movie screens across North America,
turned out to be one of the year's biggest hits, bringing in $42 million (U.S.) in its opening weekend. It
also turned out to be one of the year's best movies,
period. It won the Academy Award in the new category of best animated feature. It deserved, but did not
get, a nomination in the best picture category.

Of course, the actors are never seen on screen, since
this is a totally animated movie—a digital, high-end,
state-of-the-art animation movie. Yet the voices of the
principals—Mike Myers, Eddie Murphy, Cameron
Diaz and John Lithgow—are so familiar and so effective that their star power was one of the picture's
selling points.

The hero is a green, ugly ogre with a name that's
Yiddish for fear. He starts out feeling discontent with
being an ogre but winds up accepting himself. The
character was created by author William Steig in his
1990 children's book about a monster who's tickled to
be so repulsive. Myers plays the part brilliantly, with a
Scottish accent. And with tremendous wit and brio,

the movie turns conventional fairy tales on their heads, taking cheery satirical swipes at many contemporary institutions, especially the world of Disney. Among the comic targets: Disney's idea of a perfect civilization, Disney's depiction of fairy-tale characters, insipid Disneyland songs like "It's a Small World," and even the parking lot at Disneyland.

Shrek is a weird, funny-looking guy with big jug ears, but he also happens to be smart, kind and pensive. And that's the point: Fairy tales in which good looks are equated with nobility of character have been filling our heads with lies for centuries.

But *Shrek* delivers that message in such a stylish, entertaining way that it's utterly irresistible.

The movie's success represented sweet revenge for Katzenberg, the high-profile former employee of the Magic Kingdom who left after an ugly battle with ex-boss Michael Eisner. Along the way, Katzenberg got into a legal battle with Disney and wound up collecting a $250-million settlement. But his biggest triumph was to create sensationally popular cartoon movies that would turn Disney executives green with envy.

In *Shrek*, there's an Eisner-like ruler called Farquaad (the voice of Lithgow) who's determined to turn his kingdom, Duloc, into the most perfect, supersanitized place on earth. Consequently, he exiles a bunch of irritating fairy-tale characters, including a loquacious beast of burden called Donkey (the voice of Eddie Murphy in one of his most hilarious turns).

This is how it happens that Shrek, a privacy-loving ogre, finds his swamp overrun with these weird refugees. He makes his displeasure known to the tyrannical Farquaad, who offers a deal: Shrek can have his swamp back if he rescues the princess he hopes to marry from a dragon-guarded castle.

Katzenberg had originally planned to use Chris Farley in the role of Shrek, but after Farley's shocking death in 1998, he turned to another comedian who had become famous on *Saturday Night Live*.

On the first go-round, Myers played Shrek with his normal Canadian accent, but he wasn't satisfied with the results.

"I'm very proud to be Canadian and everybody was happy with how it turned out," he explained in pre-release interviews, "but I knew I could give more to it."

The key, he suddenly realized, was his mother, and the way she used to read fairy tales to him when he was a child.

"My mum is from Liverpool, England," Mike explained. "She's a trained actress. When I was a kid, she used to read fairy tales to me. The bookmobile would come by, and fairy tales would be in the back of the bookmobile. My mum would read all the different parts. So to me, all children's books and fairy tales have English accents. Curious George is from London. Babar is from Liverpool."

Mike realized that what was wrong with his work in *Shrek* was that he'd failed to make the connection to his mum. Once he made it, all sorts of possibilities opened up.

But wasn't it too late? Myers begged Katzenberg to let him do all his voice work over. Astonishingly, Katzenberg agreed—even though the cost of doing so was about $4 million (U.S.).

That's how it came to pass that this ogre has a slight Scottish accent—like a character who had left Scotland and immigrated to Canada 20 years ago.

In case there were any remaining doubts that Mike Myers had the Midas touch—Dietergate or no Dietergate—the phenomenal success of *Shrek* eliminated them. As an ogre who learns the secret of happiness, Mike had effectively laughed off his critics.

19

GOLDMEMBER

IN EARLY SEPTEMBER 2001, a press release from
New Line Cinema finally made it official. A new Mike
Myers movie to be entitled *Austin Powers in Goldmember*
would start production in November and be released
on July 26, 2002. Apart from *Shrek*, in which Myers was
not actually seen on the screen, this would by the comedian's first movie in three long years. Not for the first
time, Mike was going to be the Comeback Kid.

For months, the industry had been abuzz with
reports that Myers was working on a script for a third
Austin Powers movie.

New Line was committed to having its Myers movie out for the summer of 2002, and it wasn't hard to understand why. *Austin Powers: The Spy Who Shagged Me* had become the second most profitable movie in the history of the company, winding up with a cumulative worldwide gross of $310 million (U.S.).

But given what happened when Universal and Imagine had tried to rush Myers with *Dieter*, was New Line's timetable realistic? It turned out the answer was a resounding yes.

New Line's announcement confirmed details everyone in Hollywood already knew: that screenwriter Michael McCullers and director Jay Roach were also on board for the project.

This time, Myers would not only reprise his previous roles as Austin, Dr. Evil and Fat Bastard; he would also play the role of the the arch-illain Goldmember, clearly patterned on the character Goldfinger in the 1964 James Bond film of the same name.

"It's the most interesting, exotic villain people have seen in a long time," Roach told *Variety*. "Every time Mike lapsed into the character in readings, we would literally lose it and take time to regain our composure."

Other details dropped into place later. Austin's chief romantic interest this time would is Foxxy Cleopatra, played by Beyoncé Knowles, the Destiny's Child singer, sporting an amusingly large Afro. And the great veteran English actor/comedian Michael Caine plays Austin's father, Nigel, a role—for which, according to earlier rumors, the original James Bond, Sean Connery, had been wooed. Nigel is the key figure driving the plot. In this instalment, Austin, previously time-traveling between the 1960s and 1990s, drops in on the mid-1970s in order to save Nigel, who has been kidnapped by Dr. Evil.

The third Austin Powers movie also features a number of celebrity cameos, including Tom Cruise, Steven Spielberg, Gwyneth Paltrow, Britney Spears, Kevin Spacey and Katie Couric. As well, Michael York, Robert Wagner, Seth Green, Mindy Sterling and Verne Troyer reprise the roles they played in previous installments.

Austin Powers in Goldmember may be slightly less enjoyable than the first two movies in the series, and it wasn't destined to appear on any "Ten Best" lists. But it does maintain a state of blissful silliness, with enough infantile laughs to keep Myers fans happy.

The movie's biggest flaw: failing to take advantage of Michael Caine's involvement. He's hardly given anything to do.

It's greatest triumph: the hilarious opening sequence, an elaborate Hollywood inside joke that ranks as a classic of comedy history.

In January 2002, two months into filming, Austin

Powers ran into a major obstacle when MGM, which owns the James Bond franchise, petitioned the Motion Picture Association of America to stop New Line from using the title *Goldmember*.

Unless the MPAA stepped in to block New Line's plans, MGM solemnly argued, there would be a blatant infringement of MGM's copyright.

Clearly, somebody wasn't getting the joke. Ever heard of a parody?

The MPAA sided with MGM.

This wasn't the first battle MGM had waged on this front. In 1999, it had tried to stop New Line from using the title *The Spy Who Shagged Me*, but New Line won that battle. And back in 1994, MGM had had a Honda commercial driven off the airwaves because it was considered a violation of the Bond copyright.

Now in the wake of the MPAA's decision, a lot of people were stunned. The big topic of conversation all over Los Angeles: How many millions it would cost New Line to pull 11,000 trailers, thousands of posters and various other promotional materials, all prominently featuring the *Goldmember* title.

The favorite joke of the moment was that *Austin Powers 3* would henceforth be called "the movie formerly known as *Goldmember*."

Then in mid-April, after two months of heavy negotiations, came word of a settlement. MGM had agreed to allow New Line to use *Goldmember* as its title, according to a humorless joint statement.

There was something more than slightly silly about all this public agonizing and negotiating over a comedian's right to poke fun at a movie icon, and the joint statement sounded almost like a spoof.

But when it came to unintended satire, even the Goldmember title fiasco could not compete with an announcement that had come out of Universal City a month earlier.

In March, Universal Pictures proudly announced that Mike Myers had been signed to star as a famously mischievous feline visitor in a striped stovepipe hat. Mike had agreed to play the title role in a live-action adaptation of Dr. Seuss's *The Cat in the Hat*. It would be produced by Brian Grazer of Imagine Entertainment and directed by Bo Welch from a screenplay written by Alec Berg, David Mandel and Jeff Schaffer. Principal photography was to begin in the fall of 2002.

First published in 1957, *The Cat in the Hat* remains one of the top 10 best-selling children's books of all time.

Clearly, this was the project that replaced *Dieter,* with Grazer and Welch again part of the team. And just the way Jeffrey Katzenberg had arranged the deal, Universal and Imagine would be partnering on this project with DreamWorks.

But what about all the nasty things Universal and

Imagine had to say about Myers during the *Dieter* lawsuits? What about the way they had painted the comedian as a more heinous monster than Shrek, Dr. Evil and Goldmember all rolled into one?

Forget it. That's from an old, discarded script.

Stacey Snider, chairman of Universal Pictures, had this to say: "We are absolutely thrilled to be bringing another treasured Seuss story to the screen with the comic genius of Mike Myers. He will make a brilliant Cat."

During the 20-week shoot, Myers had to spend three hours a day in makeup. Part of the transformation involved a prosthetic augmentation. The movie is scheduled to open just before Thanksgiving, 2003.

In a mutual-admiration joint statement, Mike Myers and Brian Grazer explained: "The conflicts over *Dieter* are long behind us and only served to strengthen the relationship we've enjoyed for more than 10 years. We are all so enthusiastic about this project, and thrilled to have this opportunity to work together."

Translation: Universal and DreamWorks expect Dr. Seuss to make way more money than *Dieter* ever could have.

And so they're holding hands and walking into the sunset in the kind of deeply affecting happy ending that leaves everyone grinning and fighting back tears at the same time.

Welcome to Hollywood.

FILMOGRAPHY

Wayne's World (1992)
directed by Penelope Spheeris

So I Married an Axe Murderer (1993)
directed by Thomas Schlamme

Wayne's World 2 (1993)
directed by Stephen Surjik

Austin Powers: International Man of Mystery (1997)
directed by Jay Roach

54 (1998)
directed by Mark Christopher

Austin Powers: The Spy Who Shagged Me (1999)
directed by Jay Roach

Mystery, Alaska (1999)
directed by Jay Roach

Shrek (2001)
directed by Andrew Adamson and Vicky Jenson

Austin Powers in Goldmember (2002)
directed by Jay Roach

SOURCES

BOOKS

Among the books I consulted:

Myers, Mike and Robin Ruza. *Wayne's World: Extreme Close-up*. New York: Hyperion, 1991.

Patinkin, Sheldon. *The Second City: Backstage at the World's Greatest Comedy Theater*. Naperville, Ill.: Sourcebooks, 2000.

Sweet, Jeffrey, ed. *Something Wonderful Right Away*. New York: Avon Books, 1978. This is a book of oral history which includes a history of the Second City and the Compass Players.

VIDEOS

Among the material I saw on video: many sketches from *Saturday Night Live;* episodes of *It's Only Rock 'n' Roll; King of Kensington; Range Rider and the Calgary Kid;* Mike Myers on *Inside the Actors Studio.*

RADIO ARCHIVES

Among the tapes I consulted at CBC Radio archives, interviews with Vicki Gabereau in 1985 and 1986 were especially useful.

NEWSPAPERS AND MAGAZINES

Among the print publications included in my research files:

The Arizona Republic
Chicago Sun-Times
Chicago Tribune
Drama-Logue
Entertainment Today
Entertainment Weekly
eye weekly
The Globe and Mail
GQ
The Guardian (London)

The Herald (Glasgow)
The Hollywood Reporter
The Independent (London)
Knight-Ridder News
  Service
Liverpool Echo
The Los Angeles Times
Maclean's
The Nation
National Post
New York
New York Observer
The New York Times
The New Yorker
Newsday
Newsweek
Now
NY Mirror
People
Premiere
Rolling Stone
Southam News Service
The Sunday Times
  (London)
Time
Time Out (London)
The Times (London)
Toronto Life
The Toronto Star
The Toronto Sun
TV Guide
Us
USA Today
Variety

Village View
Village Voice
Wall Street Journal

INTERNET

Among the most useful
Internet sources I used
were Canoe; Dow Jones
Interactive; and Mr
Showbiz.

LIBRARIES

I made extensive use of
several libraries:

Museum of Broadcasting,
New York
Margaret Herrick Library,
operated by the Academy
of Motion Picture Arts and
Sciences in Century City,
California
Metro Reference Library,
Toronto, Ontario
CBC archives in the
Broadcast Centre,
Toronto, Ontario
Reference library of
Cinematheque Ontario,
Toronto
Library of *The Toronto
Star*

ACKNOWLEDGMENTS

It was Cynthia Good, president and publisher of the publishing division of Penguin Books, who came up with the idea for this book, and refused to take no for an answer. I am deeply indebted as well to other members of the Penguin team (which operates with almost frightening efficiency), especially Editorial Director Diane Turbide, who edited the book, and Managing Editor Tracy Bordian, who oversaw its production.

This book could not have been written without the support and encouragement of John Ferri, entertainment editor of the *Toronto Star*, who put up with having a columnist known for having his name linked to the phrase "will return."

Beverley Slopen, my agent, demonstrated the power of meaningful silence to overcome all obstacles, and kept her friendly nagging to a discreet minimum.

I'm grateful to a number of people who shared with me memories of their association with Mike Myers: Mark Breslin, John Brunton, Cory Cross, Judy Dryland, David Ferry, Ken Finkleman, Allan Guttman, Charna Halpern, Bruce Hunter, Linda Kash, Joe Kertes, Mark Lappano, Mark McKinney, Bob Reid and Al Waxman.

Joan Cohen in Los Angeles and Joshua Knelman in Toronto were hugely helpful in compiling research files. The entire staff of the *Toronto Star* library provided backup on many occasions, as did the staff of the Cinematheque Ontario library. Roy Harris was good enough to unlock the CBC vaults for me again, as he has in the past.

Sharon Kirsch, our copy editor, made many improvements.

Bernadette Sulgit, my partner in parenting, real estate and other ventures, overlooked my failure to grasp the urgency of domestic details like packing and moving.

INDEX